An African Popular Literature: A Study of Onitsha Market Pamphlets

An African Popular Literature

A STUDY OF
ONITSHA MARKET PAMPHLETS

EMMANUEL OBIECHINA

Lecturer in English, University of Nigeria, Nsukka

CAMBRIDGE

AT THE UNIVERSITY PRESS 1973

Published by the Syndics of the Cambridge University Press
Bentley House, 200 Euston Road, London NW1 2DB
American Branch: 32 East 57th Street, New York, N.Y. 10022
East African Office: P.O. Box 30583, Nairobi, Kenya
West African Office: P.M.B. 5181, Ibadan, Nigeria

The author and publishers are grateful to the authors and publishers of the material contained in the appendix to this book for allowing their work to be reproduced.

Library of Congress Catalogue Card Number: 72 83668

ISBN: 0 521 20015 6 cloth bound
0 521 09744 4 paper bound

Printed in Great Britain by
C. Tinling and Co. Ltd,
London and Prescot

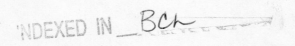

TO NNONYE, NNEKA AND IKENNA

Contents

Foreword

Since Ulli Beier first drew the attention of the literary world and of Africanists to the amazing pamphlet literature of the Onitsha Market about ten years ago in the *Times Literary Supplement,* a good many scholarly studies of it have been made and published. This is as it should be, for it is indeed a phenomenon of consuming interest whether as literature or as sociology.

I am convinced that such a literature could only have begun in Onitsha in whose ancient emporium the people of Olu and Igbo – the riverine folk and the dwellers of hinterland forests – met in guarded, somewhat uneasy commerce; the original site of evangelical dialogue between proselytising Christianity and Igbo religion, between strange-looking harbingers of white rule and (at first) an amused black population; the ground where old-time farmers met new urban retail traders; the occult no-man's-land between river-spirits and mundane humans. Onitsha had always attracted the exceptional, the colourful and the bizzare. There was the madman who reported back to his hinterland village after what must have been a bewildering visit to Onitsha that everything there (everything of the white man, that is) was blind, and proceeded to count off on his fingers: office, police, matches, Alice, notice.* Or take the stranger Englishman, J. M. Stuart-Young, scholar, trader, single-handed fighter against the new European cartels; a legend among the Igbo (for was he not a lover of the wealth-giving mermaid-queen of the Niger River?). They called him Odeziaku – Arranger of wealth; a mystery man who was perhaps a doctor of philosophy and perhaps not. Or that half-mad Okoli Ukpor whom I remember with the memory of childhood playing for money on his flute and whistling alternately a most prosaic song: 'Man and woman, whoever holds money, let him bring!' Not much of a song, perhaps, but how appropriate to his day! Occasionally he would raise an additional laugh and an additional penny by blowing his nose into the open gutter, twice, in time with his beat. Rumour had it that Okoli was as sober as you and I, had two wives and a barn full

* Each word ends in 'isi', meaning blindness.

of yams in his hinterland home and only came down to Onitsha during the slack moments on the farms to raise quick cash from amused charity by pretending to be light-headed. If that was true (and even if it wasn't) where else would such as he go but to Onitsha, where the simple mutual-trust, village economy was yielding place to a new, somewhat intoxicating, somewhat unscrupulous cash nexus? Onitsha was the nursery of an emerging Igbo capitalism – a capitalism tempered by the still strong traditional kindred concerns of the extended family. It was a place of day schools and night schools, mission schools and private schools, grammar schools and commercial schools, of one-room academies and backyard colleges. It was a self-confident place where a man would not be deterred even by insufficient education from aspiring to improve his fellows.

Dr Obiechina's study of the Onitsha pamphlet phenomenon is the fullest and the most serious so far. It relates the literature appropriately to the social ferment of the times, and is as delightful to read as the pamphlets themselves. Dr Obiechina takes the authors and their works seriously enough not to want to give them patronising praise at every turn but where necessary to question some of their social prescriptions, for example in the ever-recurring subject of love and marriage. This seriousness is necessary because the authors are concerned not to provide exotic entertainment but to tackle seriously in the light of their own perception the social problems of a somewhat mixed-up but dynamic, even brash, modernizing community. In this connection Dr Obiechina's comparison of this literature with similar phenomena is Elizabethan and eighteenth-century England is apt and revealing.

Chinua Achebe *Institute of African Studies University of Nigeria,
Nsukka, January 1973*

1   Introduction

That anyone in Nigeria should devote a whole book, even a brief one, to the popular pamphlets sold in the bookstalls of Onitsha Market shows how far we have come in taking stock of our cultural environment and recognizing the significant events within it. Until recently, when a Nigerian thought about literature, his mind immediately went to Shakespeare, Dickens, Jane Austen, Chaucer, and the other English authors whose works, for several decades, formed the only texts of English literature courses in schools and universities. Since the 1960s, however, a few African authors have found a place in the English literature syllabuses. For an increasing number of Nigerians the limits of literature have had to be extended to accommodate the works of these African writers who include Chinua Achebe, Wole Soyinka, Christopher Okigbo, John Pepper Clark, Gabriel Okara, James Ngugi, Lenrie Peters and George Awoonor-Williams. These authors have a position of honour as literary artists, not so the scores of popular pamphlet authors who began writing slightly earlier than they and have continued to produce reading material for a popular audience ever since. The idea that their works are also literature is one which the average local reader still finds hard to absorb.

But the situation is changing, thanks to the work of literary historians whose standpoint relieves them of much of the prejudices of the ordinary reader. The different segments of society have different tastes, especially in the matter of what each reads. The middle classes determine their own literary interests just as working people seek their own level of literary enjoyment. It is one function of the literary historian to recognize and record and analyse existing cultural tastes without prejudice, establishing the connectedness and underlying unity in the cultural situation.

Literary historians have done much to establish popular market literature as an integral, if unique and startling, part of the West African creative scene. A good many literary moles with a sensitive nose for what is new and significant in the creative field have burrowed into the ground covered by the pamphlet literature. The field has not been a monopoly of literary moles alone. It has since attracted others of a more or less specialized kind, social anthropologists and sociologists, political scientists and even psychologists.

Interest in this kind of writing took time to develop. The first popular pamphlets appeared in Onitsha in 1947, but it was not until fifteen years later that commentaries on them began to appear. Enthusiasm quickly built up once initial critical notice was taken. A large body of essays, reviews and commentaries bears testimony to the enthusiasm roused and sustained by the pamphlet literature once its significance was recognized.

The first such notice in a serious journal was an article called 'Writing in West Africa: A Chance to Adapt and Experiment', which appeared in the *Times Literary Supplement* of 10 August 1962. The article was not signed, as is the practice of *Times Literary Supplement*, but it has since become known that Professor Ulli Beier was the author. This is not surprising, given his interest in Nigerian art, culture and literature. The article struck certain notes which were to be repeated by subsequent reviewers and commentators. He drew attention to the spontaneity and freshness of the writing, the bold experimental spirit of the authors and the closeness of the world of the pamphlets to the broad experiences of the emergent urban working class of Nigeria. Later, he made a more detailed survey of the pamphlets in another article, 'Public Opinion on Lovers: Popular Nigerian Literature Sold in Onitsha Market', which was published in *Black Orpheus* of 14 February 1964.

Other commentaries have since appeared. Some of them are broad surveys more concerned to show the variety and general features of the writing than to explore specific themes or the technical qualities of individual works. To this category belong Donatus Nwoga's 'Onitsha Market Literature', *Transition*, IV, 19 (1965); Nancy Schmidt's 'Nigeria: Fiction for the Average Man', *Africa Report*, x, 8 (August 1965); Thomas Buckman's 'Bookstalls in an African Market: Onitsha, Eastern Nigeria', *Books and Libraries at the University of Kansas*, IV, 2 (31 November 1966); J. O. Reed's 'Africa's Market Literature', *Nation*, 196 (15 June 1963); Eugene de Benko's 'Onitsha Market Literature in the Michigan State University Library', *African Urban Notes*, II, 2 (1967); Peter Young's 'A Note from Onitsha', *Bulletin of the Association for African Literature in English*, 4 (March 1966) and S. O. Mezu's 'The Cradles of Modern African Writing', *The Conch*, II, 1 (March 1970).

Other students of the Onitsha Market pamphlets have provided more specialized studies. Some of them have explored in detail specific features of the pamphlets; others have taken up, singly or in clusters, recurrent themes in a number of pamphlets. The most important special studies are Professor H. R. Collins' *The New English of Onitsha Chapbooks* (a monograph; Ohio, 1968), Gene Ulansky's 'Caesar Crosses the River Niger: Shakespeare and Onitsha Market Chapbooks', *Journal of the New African Literature and the Arts*, 4 (1968) and Bernth Lindfors' 'Perverted Proverbs in Nigerian Chapbooks', *Proverbium*, 15 (1970), all of which are concerned with the linguistic peculiarities of the pamphlet literature. Among the themes which have been given extended treatment is politics. Professor K. W. J. Post handles it in his fascinating essay, 'Nigerian Pamphleteers and the Congo', *Journal of Modern African Studies*, II, 3 (1964). The theme is also dealt with by Bernth Lindfors in 'Heroes and Hero-Worship in Nigerian Chapbooks', *Journal of Popular Culture*, I, 1 (1967). Lindfors has also written a short paper on 'Nigerian Chapbook Heroines' for *Journal of Popular Culture*, II, 3 (1968), to which Nancy Schmidt wrote a rejoinder called 'Nigerian Chapbook Heroines: A Reply to Bernth Lindfors'.

This variety of contributions to the discussion, coupled with the fact that a number of postgraduate research workers are investigating the different aspects of the market literature, suggests that there must be something in the writing to justify all the interest. All of these essays, reviews and commentaries indicate that there is much in the pamphlets for those interested in the culture, life and society of modern Africa and how these are reflected in literature by local popular authors.

Some general statements about the form and content of the pamphlets have been published, and so have detailed studies of some aspects of the writing. This book attempts to go further. It undertakes to provide a fuller and more detailed discussion of the pamphlet literature, to explore its main themes and the major conditioning influences.

Pamphlet literature first appeared in the market town of Onitsha. In 1947, Tabansi Bookshop, a local book-selling company, published two booklets by Cyprian Ekwensi. The first, called *Ikolo the Wrestler and Other Igbo Tales*, was a collection of Igbo folktales, while the second, *When Love Whispers*, was a romantic love story. These were followed in the same year by two short stories in a booklet called *Tragic Niger Tales*. The author, Chike Okonyia, was a local school-master in Onitsha, and his stories dealt with the evil consequences of marriage by proxy. These pamphlets were instantly popular. They were widely read and discussed, especially among young grammar school boys and girls. Other pamphlets soon joined them, and other pamphlet authors quickly appeared. The production of pamphlet literature soon involved a swarm of people in the different functions of publications: authors, promoters, publishers, printers, distributors. Pamphlet publishing became a booming industry, so that, by the early 1960s, any active collector swooping down on Onitsha Market might be rewarded with as many as two hundred different titles. The printing of the pamphlets was later to spread from Onitsha to Aba, Port Harcourt, Enugu and the other towns of eastern Nigeria, and even beyond. The Onitsha main market, however, remained the chief centre of the pamphlet trade, attracting to itself pamphlets produced as far afield as Sapele, Ibadan and Lagos.

That the pamphlet literature should have developed in Onitsha is understandable. Onitsha had both natural and historical advantages making it an ideal centre of a nascent literary activity.

I have in a long introduction to an anthology of the pamphlet literature, *Onitsha Market Literature* (Heinemann Educational Books, London, 1972), described in some detail the factors which gave rise to popular pamphleteering in Onitsha. Among the factors I stressed is the favourable natural location of Onitsha as gateway to the densely-populated eastern hinterland and as a point of contact between this hinterland and the rich mid-western and western Nigeria. This led to the establishment of the first base of operation by early European missionaries and traders there, and the great impor-tance of the town as an educational and commercial centre. Other factors include the tremendous spurt in the growth of literacy after the second world war, the growth in the urban population of Onitsha, the spread in locally-owned and operated printing presses, the diversion of much energy and money previously devoted to the war effort to commercial, industrial and technological development, the significance of Onitsha main market as the commercial mart of eastern Nigeria, the influx in the 1940s of Indian and Victorian drugstore pulp magazine fiction which became a model for the pamphlet literature, and a flourishing of what could be vaguely called the 'democratic' spirit, leading to a highly developed sense of human awareness and the insistence of individuals on the relevance of their feelings and relationships.

This last point about the growth of a democratic spirit deserves further elaboration, because it would appear to explain why the pamphlet literature did not emerge in the coastal towns of West Africa, which had a highly developed literate culture several decades before the hinterland.

For a hundred years an indigenous intellectual elite, some of whose members had been educated in higher institutions in England, dominated the intellectual life of the coast. Its members had produced sophisticated literature of all sorts, from serious historical and philosophical works to anthropological and polemical essays, newspapers and journals. Whilst this coastal elite continued to be prominent and to dictate taste, the masses were unable to break down its solid wall of prejudice against 'low forms of creation', or to produce a literature adequate to their experiences. As long as this black elite which was self-conscious of its Western learning and Victorian elegances held sway, it intimidated the less educated and fended off efforts by the common people to participate in the culture over which it presided.

In the hinterland, especially in the Igbo areas, the situation was more propitious. Here, the absence of a black intellectual aristocracy made it possible for newly educated men and women to feel free to enter into full participation in the evolving modern culture without too many inhibitions. Even when an educated middle class began to emerge in the 1930s, and especially in the war years, its members shared to a large degree the provincial background of the broad hinterland masses. Some of them, like Dr Azikiwe and Mbonu Ojike, were American graduates who brought back with them an egalitarian outlook inculcated by their American education. They used their knowledge, skills and professional expertise to promote popular education and literature by setting up private and community schools and by establishing newspapers which threw their pages open to all, including the army of new literates hungry for the opportunity to air its opinion and publish its creative work. The popular newspapers, especially those set up by Dr Azikiwe from the late 1930s, became a training ground for some of the pamphlet authors.

Azikiwe's contribution to popular journalism, and its impact on the overall development of cultural awareness at the popular level, among the large body of emerging new literates, has been faithfully described by Increase Coker, a veteran Nigerian journalist. Contrasting his specifically popularizing style from 'the tradition of the 1920s when newspaper writing was confined almost exclusively to the local 'aristocracy' of intelligence, a hard-core of Sierra Leonean and other 'native foreigners' who were brought up under Edwardian and late Victorian influences', Mr Coker writes:

> An important landmark was reached on November 22, 1937, when the *West African Pilot* was launched as a daily newspaper in Lagos by Nnamdi Azikiwe. He had edited the *African Morning Post* at Accra, Gold Coast, from 1934 to 1937. Educated in America, he had graduated in political science and anthropology. He had undergone a Diploma course in Journalism at a higher institution and had actually engaged in journalistic work as City Reporter and Feature Writer. He therefore brought into the Nigerian Press brand-new ideas of newspaper writing and presentation.
>
> For the first time a measure of sensationalism was introduced into the Nigerian Press. For the first time the daily newspaper run entirely by Nigerians had come to stay as the most powerful section of the Press. Emphasis on human interest angle of general news reporting and the dramatic elements in sports stories, set the pace for the contemporaries of the *Pilot*. Politics remained the chief subject as ever it had been, but the *Pilot* introduced new life into features of general interest, such as the Women's Page, the Gossip Column, the Book Review and the Short Story. Some of these had also been introduced by the older *Nigerian Daily Times*. But the *Pilot* brought an entirely new emphasis on aspects which had almost completely been ignored by its predecessors, namely, the human interest angle of evaluating the news in anything, and the bold spirit of adventure in reporting and editorial comments . . . Lastly, a measure of pictorial journalism was brought into play by the *Pilot*. For the first time the smiling face of a Third Class Clerk in the Government or commercial houses appeared side by side with that of a lawyer or politician.
>
> ('The Nigerian Press: 1929–1959' in
> *The Press in West Africa,* Ibadan, Nigeria, 1960, p. 77.)

More important from the point of view of the popularizing and democratizing trends in the press, was the fact that the *Pilot* experiment proliferated all over southern Nigeria. In quick succession, Azikiwe set up other newspapers. The *Eastern Nigerian Guardian,* the first daily newspaper in eastern Nigeria, appeared in Port Harcourt in 1940, the *Nigerian Spokesman* at Onitsha in 1943, the *Southern Nigerian Defender* at Warri also in 1943, and the *Comet* in 1944. Each of these papers provided a platform for new writers who would not have had the confidence or the opportunity to be published in the previous decades.

The emergence of the pamphlet literature should therefore be seen as an extension of trends which were already developing in the press. Once ordinary people could be published in the newspapers, it became clear that, if there was a publishing outlet which could handle full-length works, they could also be published independently. And it was Onitsha and its Market which possessed the necessary facilities, which made it inevitable that the pamphlet literature should develop there.

The cultural and psychological outlook of the inhabitants of that boisterous town was one of the key factors that led to the emergence of the pamphlet literature. The strategic position of the town attracted people from different parts of Nigeria into it, but by far the preponderating proportion of the inhabitants remained and still remain Igbo, from both sides of the Niger River. The pamphlet business was carried on mainly by Igbo printers and publishers. The printing press owners were Igbo businessmen and the writers were, with a few exceptions, Igbo people. It would therefore be unrealistic in any discussion of the rise of the pamphlet literature to ignore local factors and the social, cultural and psychological factors which, in the final analysis, were probably the most powerful determinants.

The cultural background of the Igbo and the nature of their aspiration to modernity reveal deep, democratic impulses which contributed considerably to the emergence of the pamphlet literature. Moreover Igbo authors also contributed enormously to the development of the novel in Nigeria, Cyprian Ekwensi who was both the first Nigerian novelist and an Igbo from the locality of Onitsha pioneered the pamphlet literature. This offers us a vital indication. The Igbo, according to some social scientists, have an open, egalitarian, achievement-oriented native culture which permitted them to slide with the minimum of adjustment into modern situations and to adapt readily to the requirements of new, unusual experience. They have single-mindedly embraced modern literacy, absorbed modern skills and travelled extensively in search of work and self-sufficiency. Their physical, intellectual and social mobility is matched by the dynamic, adventurous spirit which drives them to explore new experience and to master new and challenging tasks. The American anthropologist, Ottenberg, has spoken of 'Igbo Receptivity to Change'. Other commentators like James Coleman and Margaret Green have expressed the same view. Here literary history stands to gain from the insights provided by other branches of scholarship. These sociological insights suggest that the pamphlet literature and the novel are forms whose very novelty presented them to young educated Igbo writers as an aspect of the challenge of modernity that must be met.

This point can easily be reinforced. Both the popular pamphlet literature, such as that of Onitsha Market, and the novel are a product of a highly mobile consciousness, a consciousness most actively creative where the importance of individuals is recognized and promoted within the social structure. Only to those who accept this belief in the value of the individual could such otherwise anonymous little people as office messengers, petty traders, band-leaders, students, peasant farmers, unskilled labourers, artisans, white collar workers assume sufficient importance to become the subject for literature, and for their lives and problems to engage the attention and interest of writers. It is the overwhelming concern for individuals as people, and the significance of what happens to them which has given such force to both the pamphlet literature and the novel. In both forms, this heightened awareness of individuality and the cogency of individual experience is derived partly from the modern impulses resulting from education, urbanization and technology, and partly from forces strongly lodged in the native Igbo tradition.

In other words, commentators like the English literature students of the University of Ibadan, who have sought to discover a relationship between the rise of the pamphlet literature in Onitsha and the fact that more than two-thirds of the Nigerian novelists are Igbo authors most of whom come from Onitsha and suburbs, may well be right.* Even though the popular authors write for a local, literate mass-audience and have their works printed locally, while the novelists write for a

* See the controversy in *Nigeria Magazine,* 81 (June 1964) and 82 (September 1964).

sophisticated local and overseas market and have been published in the United Kingdom, the same impulses appear to be at work in both cases. The interest in people which led Achebe to explore the personal and social predicaments of the characters in his novels probably urged Okenwa Olisa towards using the pamphlets to interpret the aspirations of young men and women in the modern world. The same democratic and adventurous spirit is at work; the different forms and techniques adopted reflect differences in education, literary exposure and intellectual orientation.

In quite another sense, the existence of popular pamphleteering in Onitsha has had an important bearing on the emergence of the novel in Nigeria. We cannot establish between them the same type of intimate connection as held between the eighteenth-century English chapbooks and Grub Street pamphleteering and the rise of the English novel; but we can at least establish an oblique influence. The existence of popular writing is a sign of a general literary awakening of which the novel is one of the highest achievements. The fact that this mass of home-produced literature is the work of people with relatively meagre formal education must have greatly encouraged the better educated and literarily inclined Nigerians to go a step further than the popular writers and produce literature of a more elevated kind. In other words, the existence of literature for the masses acted as a spur to intellectually sophisticated Nigerians to produce more sophisticated forms of literature for more sophisticated readers.

2   Literature for the Masses

Any literature which appeals to the masses must have at least three predictable characteristics: it must be simple in language and technique; it must be brief; and it must be cheap.

Simplicity and accessibility go together. The works should not make too great a demand on the intellectual and emotional resources of the reader. The habit of long and sustained poring over printed matter belongs to a small privileged minority trained by education and practice. Books aimed at the vast majority of the people must be brief and able to communicate their interest instantly, as minute rather than large doses of experience. Again, since the majority of people (even in highly industrialized countries but more so in underdeveloped ones) live at an economic level at which they struggle incessantly to supply basic needs, literature ranks low in their list of priorities and must be provided as cheaply as possible if they are to patronize it at all.

The Onitsha Market pamphlets are par excellence literature for the masses. They are stories about common people, by members of the same class, for everyone's enjoyment – though their keenest consumers remain the common people. Among the most devoted readers are grammar and elementary school boys and girls, lower-level office workers and journalists, primary school teachers, traders, mechanics, taxi-drivers, farmers and the new literates who attend adult education classes and evening schools. University graduates and people with post-grammar-school education tend to ignore this literature in favour of the more sophisticated novels, drama and poetry.

The pamphlet authors themselves have a fair idea of the kind of audience for which they produce, and they sometimes define this audience in the prefaces and introductions to their works. Thus, Cletus Nwosu, author of *Miss Cordelia in the Romance of Destiny*, says in the introduction to his book: 'I have made the book as simple as possible so that an average boy can enjoy it without his dictionary by his side.' A publisher's notice to Sigis Kamalu's *The Surprise Packet* states among other things:

I have in my list of customers the best literary brains . . . well read and intelligent indigenous authors, journalists and professional writers. We have turned and are busy turning out volumes of sensational pamphlets on good morals. There is no school boy or student in the whole Federation who has not read pamphlets published by me.

A Nigerian Union of Authors' certificate of suitability attached to H. O. Ogu's *How to Fall in Love With Girls* (A Drama) states simply that having gone through the manuscript, the Union 'recommends its suitability for use in schools and colleges for dramatization purposes'.

Occasionally, some of the novelettes have a broad, catholic appeal which their authors take pains to emphasize in the introduction – as in R. Okonkwo's *Never Trust All That Love You* in which the author writes: 'This booklet . . . has been edited at the request of the publisher to meet the literary taste of several readers and all lovers of novels and stories.'

The Onitsha Market pamphlets have a large audience. This is reflected in their sales figures. In a majority of cases, 3 to 4,000 copies are sold before a work goes out of print and is superseded; but the more popular of them sell several thousand copies more. Ogali A. Ogali's play *Veronica My Daughter* has recorded a sale of 60,000 copies and *The Nigerian Bachelor's Guide* by A. O. Ude, of 40,000 copies. Most of the books are printed once or twice and then go out of print but the more popular ones, like the two mentioned above, are re-issued several times and thus reach the largest body of readers.

The pamphlets sell well because they cost so little. When they first appeared in the late 1940s, they were sold for between 1*s* and 1*s* 6*d* a copy. Since then, the increased cost of production labour and newsprint has forced up prices to between 1*s* and 3*s* 6*d*. But even now, they remain within reach of most readers.

This is of course not to underrate the hard-headed monetary calculation that goes into the pamphlet enterprise. As a matter of fact, the printing and publishing of the pamphlets has developed into a major industry centred on Onitsha Market. Here, the publishers band themselves into a kind of guild with regulations and rules of conduct. They have common practices for commissioning works from would-be authors, and they have evolved entrepreneural techniques for regulating the pamphlet business and making money out of it. Initial capital outlay for purchase of a printing press, employment of the services of editors, compositors, type-setters, and so on, all come into the calculation, and so does the margin of profit which the printer-publishers expect from their undertaking. The low cost of the pamphlets is, in the long run, part of the strategy for maximizing profit.

For the authors of the pamphlets, monetary gain is of secondary importance only. Unlike the printer–publishers, the satisfaction of being seen in print is often adequate compensation to the pamphlet authors. They hold authorship in high esteem, amounting almost to awe. Cletus Nwosu in a Preface to *Miss Cordelia in the Romance of Destiny* gives the reasons why he has chosen to become an 'author' as:

(i) to write a book for the interest and amusement of all Nigerian students;

(ii) for the purpose of dedicating it [the book] to his boyhood friend and companion – Lawrence Chikwendu, and

(iii) to add his name to the list of Nigerian Authors.

The same reverential attitude to authorship is clearly shown in the first editorial of the *Nigerian Authors Magazine* (1962), an organ set up by the popular authors to serve the interest of pamphlet literature, which says: '"Author" is, in our own candid opinion, and in the opinion of those who matter in the literary field, a prouder title than "king".'

Because of the immense prestige attached to authorship and the avid desire of the pamphlet writers to appear in print, most of the authors would accept, especially for their maiden works, mere token payments of a few shillings for their manuscripts, though the better known ones receive considerable sums. Publishers could, and do, exploit the new authors' anxiety to be published by paying low fees but established authors insist on fair rewards, sometimes amounting to £10 10s for a manuscript.

Most of the pamphlet authors are, like the more sophisticated novelists and dramatists of West Africa, amateurs rather than professionals. They have some full-time occupation by which they earn their living, and they merely take up writing as a pastime. A large number of the pamphlet authors are school teachers, local printing-press owners and book sellers but a considerable number of them are also journalists, railwaymen, traders, clerks, artisans, farmers and even grammar school boys. These latter write under false names to escape detection by their school authorities, or sometimes in their real names where they have the support and sympathy of their teachers.

The authors are often encouraged by their more educated friends and kinsmen, their writers' associations, their publishers and, if students, sometimes by their teachers. These supporters express their enthusiasm by contributing more or less commendatory prefaces to the finished works. They sometimes include in the prefatory notes much biographical information about the authors, as well as furnishing such details as how and why the authors came to be involved in pamphlet writing.

The relationship between the authors and the publishers of the Onitsha Market literature is an interesting one. Publishers either commission well-known writers or insert brief advertisements in published works inviting would-be authors to send in short stories and plays, sometimes with an accompanying promise of money payment. When a manuscript has been handed in by the author and paid for by the publisher, then the author's interest in it tends to come to an end. Thus it is not unusual for such a work to carry the name of the publisher, instead of its author's. That explains why several works occasionally appear under one man's name while some others appear under fanciful borrowed names like Speedy Eric, Strong Man of the Pen, Highbred Maxwell, Money Hard and so on.

There is of course always a tacit understanding between author and publisher as to what the popular taste dictates for each story or play. At all times the interest of the popular audience is paramount, and if the writer's creative interest chances to draw him somewhat out of the direct line of the popular taste because he is not immediately aware of this taste, the publisher, with his eye on profit and the sales figures, cannot afford to ignore it. Thus it is not unusual for a publisher to give detailed specifications as to the content of a commissioned work as well as to insist that certain themes, attitudes and even forms of language be emphasized as a means of arresting popular interest. This further explains why occasionally a title on the page of a book differs, by a very wide margin, from the actual content of the work. Whenever this happens, the publisher must have used his superior 'hunch' to divine what title is best suited to arrest popular attention, regardless of what is actually contained between the covers.

Popular tastes are also decisive in determining the format of the Onitsha Market literature. Because its audience is composed largely of new literates who cannot grapple with big books, the popular authors have understandably chosen the pamphlet – a much briefer and more manageable medium than the novel. The normal pamphlet has between ten and seventy pages. Its front-cover, and sometimes its back-cover, carries striking photographs of film-stars or hand-drawn pictures illustrative of the titles. The attractive covers are meant to catch the eye, and the books sometimes contain illustrative sketches and pictures which help to enliven their contents.

The scope of the pamphlet literature is wide. Some of the pamphlets appear in Igbo, and others in English. The English ones are better known to the multi-lingual reading public of Nigeria. This tends to obscure the fact that a good many books have also been produced in Igbo and have been eagerly bought by a fair section of the reading public, especially participants in adult education.

It is no surprise that vernacular writers should flourish side by side with works written in English. The tradition of vernacular literacy in Igboland is much older than that of literacy in English; indeed, it goes back a hundred years to the setting up of a Christian missionary post in Onitsha in the mid-nineteenth century.* The proselytizing interest of the missionaries required that the Bible, liturgical works and hymns should be translated into Igbo for the benefit of new converts. To foster literacy in the Igbo language, the early missionaries had to compose grammar books and dictionaries as well as recording oral traditions, folklore, and local history in that language. All these activities led to the building up of quite a substantial Igbo reading audience long before the diffusion of literacy in English. The tradition of Igbo literacy has been sustained further by Igbo being recognized as a school subject as well as a medium of instruction in the lower levels of the primary school.

Some of the pamphlet authors who have written in English have also occasionally written in Igbo. For example, Ogali A. Ogali, one of the most prominent pamphlet authors in English, is also the author of a number of Igbo pamphlets. Two of his Igbo works, *Ilu na ọfọ na ogu nke ndi Igbo* (Igbo proverbs and ethics) and *Adanma Nwam* (Adanma my daughter, a drama) were published at the modest price

* As early as 1859 the Rev. Joseph Christopher Taylor, a C.M.S. Missionary in Onitsha had written *Isuama Ibo Katkism*. In 1860 the first Igbo Bible was published. In 1882, the Rev. Ajayi Crowther, the first C.M.S. Bishop on the Niger wrote *Vocabulary of the Ibo Language*. Earlier, another missionary, the Rev. J. F. Schon, had written an Igbo grammar titled *Oku-Ibo*.

of one shilling and sixpence at the time of the appearance of the best of his English works. Another pamphlet author and publisher, C. N. Onuoha, who goes by the pseudonym 'Moneyhard', has among his titles such popular Igbo pamphlets as *Uzo Esienyere Ndu Aka* (The way to improve one's life) and *Akuko Banyere Ogaranya na Ogbenye* (A tale of rich and poor) which cost a shilling per copy. Some of the pamphlet authors, like Okenwa Olisa in *No Condition is Perfect,* are content to insert fragments of useful knowledge, including sayings of the wise and figures of speech, for the benefit of Igbo-speaking readers.

In more recent times and with the recognition of Igbo as a standard subject in the overseas and local examinations, a spate of Igbo pamphleteering has arisen in response to the reading needs of schools and colleges. These educational and examination pamphlets in Igbo are largely the works of educationists and official examiners and have often been commissioned by local and overseas publishers or produced as a collaborative endeavour of a number of interests fostering the growth and development of vernacular literature. Here Christian missionary bodies and their publishing arms have continued to lead among agencies encouraging the growth of writing in Igbo.

Among the most interesting pamphlet works in Igbo are Pita Nwana's *Omenuko,* an exciting biography of a successful, though sardonic, slave-dealer of that name; J. A. Dureke's *Egwu Ọnwa* (Moonlight revels); K. A. Achinivu's *Ila Ọsọ Ozuakọli* (The Ozuakọli games); G. E. Igwe's *Ekeresimeesi* (Christmas); Anya Iwe's *Akukọ Ifọ Ụfọdụ Kwesiri Ka Ụmụ Mmadụ Mara* (Some folktales worth knowing). The veteran Onitsha schoolmaster, F. C. Ogbalu has both written numerous Igbo pamphlets (including the ever-popular collection of Igbo tortoise tales, *Mbediọgu*) and has also set up a publishing business that specializes in Igbo works.

The distinctly pedagogical emphasis of most of these educational and examination pamphlets in Igbo is shown by the fact that they deal with customary habits and cultural events. There is often an intention to entertain the reader, as in a good many of the popular pamphlets, but the more serious interest of imparting factual knowledge and informing the reader on specific cultural traits or customary practices is always predominant. This characteristic, and the fact that the educational Igbo pamphlets are the works of sophisticated intellectuals some of whom are graduates of the School of African and Oriental Languages, removes these works from the class of the popular pamphlets proper. In fact, they are aimed at an audience different from the one for whom the popular authors write. The army of semi-literates who devour *No Condition Is Permanent* or *Why Boys Never Trust Money Monger Girls* or *The Way to Make Friends With Girls* or even *Adanma Nwam* is bound to differ substantially from that other army, keen-eyed and meticulous, which rummages the pages of the Igbo educational pamphlets for the key with which to open the door to 'my Cantab' or 'my Wasc' (West African School Certificate). While the popular pamphlets, properly defined, are produced by local publishers and printed in Onitsha or any of the major eastern Nigerian towns, the Igbo educational pamphlets are, in most cases, produced by overseas publishers who are devoted as much to the pursuit of excellence in workmanship as to promising sales returns.

Among the pamphlets in English, some are fiction while others deal with non-fictional subjects. Among the non-fiction are those which teach the technique of examinations and others which provide advice for young men and women on how to cope with the problems of modern life, advice ranging from how to fall in love to how to launder clothes. Some booklets record local history, collections of folk-tales, proverbs and anecdotes peculiar to Igboland. The fictional ones include novelettes (often wrongly labelled 'novels' by the authors), dramas based on love and marriage, or stories about prominent Africans. Others carry tales of adventure and wonder. By far the largest group of the fictional pamphlets is concerned with love situations and marriage.

In the main, the content of the pamphlet literature reveals a preoccupation with the problems of a changing society in which the growth of new cultural elements has stimulated new desires, new attitudes and new values. The pamphlet literature articulates these sweeping changes, and attempts to provide some kind of guidance and direction to the masses of the people caught in the violence and confusion arising from the changes.

In the treatment of its major themes and interests, the Onitsha popular literature retains its popular quality of simplicity and lightness. Even when dealing with what might appear the most serious subject, its approach is hardly ever solemn. The desire to entertain and amuse is always paramount. The typical pamphlet author paints his picture with a light, comic brush. That is why the pamphlet scene is teeming with comic, ridiculous and grotesque characters and incidents. They make use of 'bombast' characters (like Bomber Billy in Ogali's *Veronica My Daughter*), 'pidgin' characters (like Chief Bombey in R. Okonkwo's *The Game of Love*) and deliberately created comic names (such as Ototofioko). These are there for their comic effect. The same desire to amuse and entertain is responsible for the melodramatic treatment of many of the situations in the pamphlets, the sensationalizing of incidents and the reinforcing of descriptions with much titillating detail. It accounts for many of the fights and the slap-stick comedy, many of the broad jokes and the vituperative name-calling, and the use of expressions and sobriquets widely current at Onitsha Market. The Onitsha Market literature partakes of the humour, the informality and the openness of life in Onitsha Market itself.

3 Passport to the Happy Life

The Onitsha Market literature is concerned with the business of living. It is about young men and women who are intensely alive and who, because they are so, have problems arising from the complexities of modern life. Most of those at whom the literature is directed have had only a superficial contact with modern ways and are in need of guidance and help if they are to cope with them.

There are in the first place the techniques of modern living which must be mastered. Then there are skills to be acquired and jobs to be held down. There is the problem of operating the modern economic machinery with its dependence on the almighty dollar. For those just emerging from peasant self-sufficiency the problem of adjustment to the new system looms large on the horizon. It is both an economic problem and a moral one.

Literacy opens the door to success and the achievement of most of the objectives of the young men and women in their aspiration to modernity. A number of the pamphlets, in response to this particular need, are therefore directed towards helping the reader to acquire new knowledge, to enable him pass examinations and improve himself generally. There are numerous titles indicating the educational interests of the pamphlets such as: *How to Write Good English and Composition*; *How to Write Better Letters, Applications and Business Letters*; *How to Succeed in Life*; *How to Know Hausa, Ibo, Yoruba and English Languages*; *How to Know Proverbs and Many Things*; *How to Make Meetings*; *Pocket Encyclopaedia of Etiquette and Commonsense*. There are also numerous texts for primary schools and popular examination-made-easy booklets on every conceivable subject.

The pedagogic interest is so seriously pursued by the pamphlet authors that in some of their works, they find space for unrelated information which may enrich a reader's knowledge. This is inserted in the final pages, usually under the heading of *Things Worth Knowing*. For example, at the end of the pamphlet telling the story of Chief Awolowo's treason trial (the pamphlet is philosophically titled *The Bitterness of Politics and Awolowo's Last Trial* and written by

Mazi Raphael Nwankwo) the publisher thoughtfully inserts the following information which has no bearing on the subject of the book but is simply worth knowing: 'The world population was said to have reached 3,180,000,000 in mid-1963. This amounts to a gain of 185 million in only three years. Of this population, the Republic of China occupies almost one quarter.' This is the kind of information provided by the United Nations statistical publications, which are not available to most people. The pamphlet literature brings it to its numerous local readers.

The wish to spread education through these books is praiseworthy, but the result has not always proved happy for the educational system as a whole. Because the pamphlets provide ready-made knowledge, readers go to them for 'reach-me-down' answers which they use parrot-wise at examinations. The love of new knowledge is almost negated by the tendency to give and receive education unthinkingly, and the habit of thinking and writing in cliches has grown with the spread of model answers and 'knowledge-without-tears' booklets.

Another group of improving pamphlets aims not at regaling the reader with knowledge, but on reforming his morals and refining his attitudes in order to prepare him to face the social, economic, and emotional problems of the present day. These pamphlets embody open or implicit didactic intentions.

Didacticism is expressed in the pamphlet literature in many ways. Often, it is in the nature of warnings against the moral dangers and pitfalls of town life, and sometimes of giving the reader, in pseudo-philosophic and sententious manner, a certain kind of insight into contemporary life. Sometimes the didacticism takes the form of cautionary tales embodying explicit and implicit lessons.

The didactic purpose is often stated in the authors' prefaces. This is one of the conventional practices in the pamphlet literature. A few typical examples will demonstrate the practice.

'There are three points that stand as key or a guide in the writer's mind', states Raphael Obioha in *Beauty is a Trouble*, 'first, to find out whether the story is educative, secondly, to see that it is entertaining, and third, to see that it is instructive.' The young grammar-school boy, John Ngoh, writes in *Florence in the River of Temptation*:

> My aim in composing this novel is to expose vice and praise
> virtue. To this end I hope my readers will find in this novel an
> unforgettable lesson which will be their guide in times of
> difficulties.

N. O. Madu writes in *Miss Rosy in the Romance of True Love:*
> The case dealt with in this story is a valuable one, and readers
> will discover for themselves that the married life of today is
> often a force, a bargain or a vulgarity rather than a great
> spiritual enterprise. This book . . . will show how far true this
> statement is. What the expressions 'I love you' and 'My dear'
> carry after them or when they come from the lips of a woman,
> can be found under the cover of this book.

Thomas Iguh warning the reader against obsession with love in
The Sorrows of Love writes:
> This novel is designed to serve as a lesson to some of our
> young boys and girls who feel that there is another heaven in
> the game of love.

S. E. Eze says simply of his book, *How to Know a Good Friend,*
> It contains important facts and gives good advice to men and
> women.

G. O. Obiaga, a pharmacist, writes in the preface to his brother,
C. C. Obiaga's novelette, *Boys and Girls of Nowadays:*
> The story is full of life, and it depicts the life of young men
> and women of Nigeria today. The moral drawn from it is
> educative, cautioning and forestalling all in one, and I hope all
> and sundry will read and enjoy this story and keep a copy of
> this interesting booklet.

Sometimes the language in which the moral purpose is stated is less
soberly prosaic, it can be extremely witty or even titillating as in
Speedy Eric's *Mabel the Sweet Honey that Flowed Away.* 'Her skin',
the author writes,
> would make your blood flow in the wrong direction. She was
> so sweet and sexy, knew how to romance. She married at
> sixteen. But she wanted more fun. Yet it ended at seventeen.
> And what an end! So thrilling.

The last remark applies to the story, of course, not to Mabel's life
which is obviously censured.

Some of the prefaces are amusing because they contain
incongruous or absurd statements. An example is in R. Okonkwo's
Never Trust All That Love You which announces that the author
> is showing modern Nigerianization . . . [and the] . . .
> capacity of educating the illiterates, who through the means
> of reading the good novels written in good English language
> learn greatly.

The assumption that illiterates can read 'the good novels' and that only they need instruction in the use of good English demonstrates the anxiety of the pamphlet authors to instruct and improve their audience. Illiteracy and the inability to communicate properly are recognized as handicaps to anyone intending to make the best of contemporary life and its opportunities.

If the writers' manifestoes read in part like tracts for the times, it is mainly because the times need tracts. The writers attempt to correct defects in contemporary society. They deal with the more immediate problems which confront the average young man and woman in the changing social situation, problems of how to make and keep money, of whether or not it is desirable to fall in love, of whether parents are justified in intervening to determine who should or should not marry their daughters and so on.

What the Onitsha pamphlet authors are doing has had parallels in other parts of the world. Writers at times of social change and the break-down of established values have always taken upon themselves part of the burden of helping people to find new values or a new synthesis in order to minimize the pains of change. Elizabethan and early eighteenth-century England offer two examples of periods in which writers using the pamphlet form attempted to provide advice and guidance for the benefit of young men and women exposed to rapid social change.

The Elizabethans through such booklets as Greene's *Notable Discovery of Cosenage* and *Groatsworth of Wit bought with a Million of Repentance* warned young Englishmen coming from the countryside into London against the wiles of pimps and prostitutes, rogues and swindlers of all sorts, as well as the evils of the taverns and such 'haunts of iniquity'. They put one in mind of J. O. Nnadozie's *Beware of Harlots and Many Friends,* Okenwa Olisa's *Drunkards Believe Bar Is Heaven.* The early eighteenth-century conduct-books of Defoe and Richardson, books such as Defoe's *The Complete English Tradesman* and Richardson's *The Apprentice's Vade Mecum: or Young Man's Pocket Companion* preferred practical advice to ordinary people on such matters as the conduct of employers and apprentices or masters and servants, how to conduct one's working life most profitably, how people could best carry on their private life, how young women could safeguard their virtue and make desirable marriages, the evils of clandestine and forced marriages, and so on. Their authors did for their time what the Onitsha pamphleteers are attempting to do for contemporary Nigerians.

Nor does the resemblance stop there. Defoe and his contemporaries, like the Onitsha Pamphlet authors, used short stories and incidents to point their morals. These *exempla,* as they were called, were at later stages collected and compiled and issued as books. An advertisement which appeared in 1736 gives an idea of the wide scope of the *exampla.* It offers: 'A choice, Instructive and very Entertaining Collection of memorable and genuine Histories.'

> This collection, which is calculated for the Entertainment of
> all Sorts of Readers, will contain a far greater Variety of
> surprising and remarkable Events than any work yet extant;
> and the tracts are generally vouched for true by the respective
> Authors. Besides many notable Instances of the ruinous
> Effects of Hatred, Lust, Envy, Avarice, Revenge, etc.
> Fortitude and their Contraries, it includes the detestable
> Lives, and deserved Punishments of a great Number of most
> notorious Murderers, Robbers, Thieves, Sharpers etc . . . Few
> books can be more useful and necessary in Families than this
> Collection, it abounds with Morality, and directing Youth to
> the Love of Virtue, as also deterring them from vicious
> Courses, by very notable Examples.

The notice, which reads rather like the manifestoes of the Onitsha Pamphlet Literature, indicates some common ground between the eighteenth-century *exempla* and the popular Onitsha pamphlets. The intentions of their authors, to reform the morals of their contemporaries by writing tales which illustrate both the recommended norms of behaviour and their condemned opposites, is certainly a common feature.

The quest for the good life is most clearly illustrated in the pamphlet literature by those authors who deal with the problem of money and material wealth.

On the level at which the popular writers perceive modern life, money is a very desirable thing. They accept that you cannot get very far without it. You need it to equip yourself with the modern necessaries of life such as household furniture, good clothes, decent meals, and the new prestige goods that raise your standing in society. If you are on the lower rungs of the economic ladder, you need money to purchase yourself a bicycle, a radio, and to get yourself a wife. On the higher economic level, you would need a motor car, a radiogram, a house, money to provide sumptuous and lavish parties as befits your dignity, and to buy gorgeous and costly clothes that symbolize your social standing. Whether you are in the higher or lower income-bracket, you need money to educate your children and the children of your close kin, and generally to help your parents and the members of your extended family out of their numerous financial problems.

To the popular authors therefore it is of the greatest importance that a man should work and earn money. They are not at all concerned, as the intellectual authors of West Africa are, whether the mere possession of money and material wealth is enough to ensure individual happiness. There is only one case in which the value represented by money is superseded by a higher value, and that is in the matter of marriage. The popular authors generally agree that when the choice is between marriage based on love and marriage based on money, the interest of love should come before that of money. Apart from this case, which is a special one, money and the values represented by it stand very high in the estimation of the popular authors. It is to them a necessary element in the individual's quest for self-fulfilment. The means of its acquisition must of course be scrupulously honest (there are many instances in the tales in which its illegal or immoral acquisition is shown to be the undoing of apparently successful men). But the ability to earn 'good' money is often pictured as both a virtue and a means to individual happiness.

The writers therefore extol hard work and frugality (which they are careful to distinguish from miserliness and meanness). 'When you are poor', writes Okenwa Olisa, one of the foremost of the didactic pamphlet authors,

> be an industrious man. Don't sit idle. You cannot win raffle when you do not sign it, it is when you sign it you will watch what will be the result. That is, you will not become rich when you do not work, it is when you work that you will begin to watch what your labour will produce. To be rich is very hard, but some people do not know. Some people think it is a thing of chance. God cannot send you a parcel of food from heaven. He can only bless and protect you. Don't imitate [the rich] when you have no money. You know that a hungry man who does not take care will eat poison, as well as a poor man who imitates [the rich] will steal.

This quotation which is headed 'Advice to Young Men About Money' is taken from Olisa's *No Condition Is Permanent*. In it we can recognize the influence of missionary education in Christian sentiments and the preacher's familiar rhetoric, particularly the elaboration of a central theme by side reference and analogies. It is an ironic piece of advice which embodies a most palpable materialistic sentiment within the framework of Christian sermonizing.

This is of course not unheard-of. The mixture of materialistic and religious sentiments was one of the major characteristics of the early eighteenth-century English conduct-books mentioned above. The virtues of diligence, thrift, sobriety and prudence promoted by Defoe and his contemporaries in their works were hallowed and sanctified by Puritan Protestantism which taught that the pursuit of wealth was not merely an advantage but a Christian duty. Max Weber's *The Protestant Ethic and the Rise of Capitalism* identifies this Puritan economic outlook with the growth of industrialism and capitalism in England. Work is portrayed in Defoe's books as a virtuous exercise, while wasting time and spending money on pleasure-conferring things were regarded as a sinful diversion from saintly living.

It is not suggested that the attitude of the Onitsha pamphleteers derives from a doctrinal basis as consistent and clearly defined as that of the English eighteenth-century Puritan pamphleteers. But enough common ground exists between the two groups of writers on the question of economic success to make the comparison fruitful. For example, Defoe's advocacy of a life of industry and action and contempt for the 'Nothing-Doing Wretch' finds echoes in many sentiments expressed in the Onitsha popular pamphlets; and so would this passage which appears in his *Complete English Tradesman*:

> The Tradesman, that is a thriving, managing, diligent Man, is
> full of Vigour, full of Vivacity, always stirring and bustling,
> never idle, never sottish; his Head and his Heart are
> employed; he moves with a kind of Velocity, unknown to
> other men. (II (1727, i. 73))

The economic attitudes of the Onitsha pamphleteers mark them out as materialists. They desire change and the innovations which change brings, including the new consumer durables. In this respect, they contrast sharply with the West African intellectual authors, most of whom tend to relate most of the ills of contemporary West African society to economic individualism and the corrupting influence of materialism. This divergence in attitudes must be traced to two essential factors: the difference in the depth of intellectual orientation between the two types of writers and their differing circumstances.

To take the first point first, it would be fair to expect that the novelists and other sophisticated authors would as intellectuals show a deeper critical awareness of the problems of society than the pamphlet writers, who see the problems mainly on the surface and very much at the personal rather than social level. The intellectual authors' attitude to material wealth is largely determined by what they see as the depraving effect of materialism on individual character. They attribute much of the sufferings of individuals to the materialism of contemporary life which some of them blame on the introduction of Western economic rationalization and materialism. The popular writers are not even remotely concerned with such lofty considerations. Having committed themselves to the modern way of life, they accept without reserve and without apology the economic consequences of this commitment. Their general attitude is more practical and more uncomplicated than the moral attitude of the intellectuals. To them, wealth is there to be possessed and enjoyed. The only thing that approaches a moral attitude to money and material possession is their insistence on the individual's proper husbanding of his resources and avoidance of excessive or imprudent spending.

The popular pamphlet writers come, on the whole, from within the lower income bracket, unlike the intellectual authors all of whom belong to the so-called 'senior service' class. The pamphleteers aspire to such items of prestige and status as bicycles, gramophones, radios, radiograms and even motor-cars; they want to own houses, to furnish their living apartments in modern style, to dress well, and generally to acquire such possessions as will enhance their standing in the eyes of their neighbours. The intellectual authors, as members of a fairly well-paid segment of society, can afford to take those possessions for granted. The clear disparity in economic position reinforces the view that the intellectual authors are disenchanted with materialism because, having tasted most of its fruits, they have come to see, and rightly too, that it does not, and cannot, provide the realization of individual happiness. The popular authors and their audience still aspire to the fruits of materialism and have not yet attained them, so they have not yet come to a stage of social or intellectual consciousness in which they could adopt a critical attitude to materialism. The junior civil servant, school-teacher or petty trader who looks at the car-owning civil servant with envy and admiration not unmixed with awe is not likely, when he turns his mind to writing about such things, to scoff at the effort of individuals to climb to higher economic positions in which they might ultimately join the rank of car-owners. As a result, where the intellectual authors see in the struggle of individuals to amass wealth a soul-destroying rat race, the popular writers see it as a proper way for the individual to raise his social standing and enhance his happiness.

The popular pamphleteers welcome the opportunities in a society which leaves the door open for the individual to get on. Their tales are full of instances of those who started life at the bottom and pulled themselves up to lofty heights of success. In most of their novelettes, everybody has a recognized and named trade or a profession, or attends school, with the purpose of preparing for a trade or a profession. Some of the chief heroes are those who go to work in the day and study for external certificates and degrees at night. They are allotted the really virtuous roles in the tales. Heroes generally prosper in their chosen occupations, but their successes and triumphs soon become failures when they allow themselves to be diverted from their serious occupations. What the evidence of their own eyes and everyday experiences shows to the popular writers is that in a ruthlessly competitive society that man is a failure (and therefore unhappy) who cannot exert himself or is foolish enough to throw away his hard-earned money.

The pamphlet writers therefore regard it as their duty to warn their readers by cautionary tales, *exempla* or anecdotes, against the evil or foolish courses through which individuals easily lose their money, especially in the towns. They single out three major sources of financial ruin to the unwary town-dweller: going after flashy, money-grabbing women; addiction to the bottle; and 'high life', or the tendency of the individual to live beyond his means. Thus, their pamphlets carry such cautionary titles as: *Money Hard To Get But Easy to Spend*; *Why Boys Never Trust Money Monger Girls*; *Drunkards Believe Bar Is Heaven*; *Beware of Harlots and Many Friends*; *Beware of Women*; *Why Harlots Hate Married Men and Love Bachelors*; *Money Hard But some Women Don't Know*; *Why Men Never Trust Women*; *Never Trust All That Love You*; *Be Careful*; *Salutation Is Not Love*.

The pamphlet writers have different techniques for putting across their economic lessons. A writer may adopt the preaching technique, in the nature of a tract for the times, in which he emphasizes the

positives of a money-making working life, as in this extract from
Okenwa Olisa's *Money Hard To Get But Easy To Spend:*

> He who seeks for money and wants to have it must not say
> that the rain is too much, he must work under it. He must not
> say that the sun is coming, he must work under it. He must
> sing his favourite song and work. He must not fear work. He
> must work hard. He must be obedient. He must be humble.
> He must be punctual to his work. He must endure insult,
> abuse. He must take trouble of many kinds. He must not play
> with his business. If a tradesman, he must be honest and
> sincere to his Customers. He must improve his handwork in
> order to attract customers. He must not charge too much. He
> must not play with his business, otherwise his business plays
> with him.

This tract is obviously directed to the small man, and not the
business executive or the high-level civil servant. It is a guide to the
apprentice, the manual worker, the artisan, the shop-keeper and
everyone within the lower income bracket. That is why there is such
emphasis on obedience, humility and honesty, sincerity and improve-
ment of handwork in order to attract customers. The man in the
executive position does not need these injunctions; rather, it is the
apprentice, the self-employed tradesman, the trader and those in
subordinate positions who need them.

It is not enough to work hard and show a clear determination to
earn. Money once earned must be prudently used or it will soon
vanish. The writers therefore sometimes list the main dangers to the
proper husbanding of money. Here, for example, is Okenwa Olisa's
list in *No Condition Is Permanent*. The section is titled 'Another
Advice to Men About Money'.

> When you have money these misbehaviours could drive it out
> and you fall woefully: pride, recklessness, carelessness,
> highlife, excess happiness, chasing badly, drunkenness,
> wickedness, enviousness, unnecessary economicals, having
> confidence in everyone, deceit and fraud, pretence, claiming
> too know and superiority, forgetting God.

The presence of some items in this formidable list is surprising, but
no doubt the author if called upon could expatiate convincingly on
why each 'misbehaviour' could prevent an individual from saving his
money or spending it in a desirable manner. The items which appear
most odd here, include 'wickedness', 'enviousness' and 'forgetting

God'. Anyone familiar with popular African beliefs will recognize the view, usually held, that a wicked or envious man never truly prospers. He may make his money by employing doubtful or immoral means, but something soon happens to rob him of his gains. A fire, thieves, costly litigation – any of these things could sweep away in a brief moment all that the evil man has immorally built up. And a man who forgets God is likely, sooner or later, to do something unwise which will end in his losing his money.

Occasionally, the point is made through a factual statement backed up with a sketched illustration, as in Olisa's *Money Hard To Get But Easy To Spend*. Here, a young labourer is shown cutting down a tree in the burning tropical sun. Next, he is pictured smartly dressed and ordering twelve bottles of beer. The author then comments disapprovingly: 'He is buying 12 bottles of beer from the shop. The cost is £1 10s. His salary is £4 10s per month, 3s per day. It takes 10 tough days to get £1 10s but takes him only 5 minutes to spend it.' This Defoe-like attention to arithmetic drives the lesson home by making it scrupulously factual, hence obvious.

Other writers handle the theme through question and answer or through dialogue. In R. Okonkwo's *Why Boys Never Trust Money Monger Girls* the following questions and answers occur:

Question: Why do boys never trust girls of the present time?
Answer: Because they are money-mongers and cannot tell the truth.
Question: Can a money-monger girl love you if you do not spend money for her?
Answer: No.
Question: Why do many girls love some ugly men?
Answer: Because they can get money from them.
Question: Is it good for you to forget your business and think of your girl friend?
Answer: It is not. No money, no girls.

Elsewhere in the same booklet a character bemoans the stupidity of men who allow themselves to be 'milked' by 'money-monger' girls. 'It is the men', he laments, 'that always put themselves into trouble. They would suffer every pain to get money, but when they get it, they couldn't think or remember all the pains they have suffered before giving it away to women.'

The following dialogue in the same booklet shows that the writer also sees idleness or too much leisure as a hindrance to prosperity. It takes place between a group of young men standing at the corner of a street.

> *Edwin*: Ha! friend, why are you standing here like a traffic police-man on duty, any news?
> *Matthew*: Just to pass away the time and also to enjoy the fine weather of today. How about things?
> *Edwin*: Which things do you mean, business or what?
> *Matthew*: I mean business which is the foundation of life.
> *Joe*: But do you have any other thing in mind as you are asking so?
> *Edwin*: Oh no, friend, I am only thinking of my business. It is business before pleasure.
> *Matthew*: You say business before pleasure. Does it mean that a businessman can't be happy?
> *Edwin*: No! Not that way, all I mean is that a person must suffer before he starts to enjoy the fruit of his or her labour.
> *Joe*: So you are trying to tell me that all people must suffer before they can start to enjoy themselves.
> *Edwin*: You know that destinies are not the same but to my own understanding I feel it is more good and wise for a person to suffer whether (he is) from a rich family or not, before he jumps to be happy.

The burden of this dialogue is that it is prudent for the individual to work hard and build himself up economically before he earns the right to live a leisurely and pleasurable life. The dialogue is contrived, because its purpose is not so much to recapture an actual conversation as to put across a particular point of view. There is a directness of attack such as we encounter in European medieval morality plays and in Bunyan's allegories.

In other cases, the economic theme is illustrated by short stories with clearly pointed morals. A typical plot describes how a young man who starts life with nothing at all works very hard to improve his economic position. When he has very nearly succeeded, he commits the supreme indiscretion of falling in love with an unscrupulous, scheming woman who proceeds to strip him of all he has so painfully garnered.

Such is the plot of C. C. Obiaga's *Boys and Girls of Nowadays*. In the story, Jerry, a young man who could not get a salaried job because he was 'a little bit educated but his education was not enough to put him into any office work' settles down to petty trading. He is

helped with capital by a kindly elder brother to whom he promises to
repay the loan as soon as his business picks up. At first Jerry makes
good progress but soon success goes to his head and he begins to live
extravagantly. This is how his new style of life is described:

> Very soon, Jerry changed his abode. He who was living in a
> filthy room now had three rooms in a storied building. His
> house was so furnished that one would see one's reflection on
> the floor and (on) the furniture in his sitting room. People
> used to say that he had the biggest radiogram in the town.
> And it was true: Lucky Jerry sewed many clothes for different
> occasions. He had upwards of five suits, many trousers,
> native dresses and all. Whenever one came to his house,
> music would be booming from the radiogram. He was as
> happy as could be. And who wouldn't.

The last remark has a somewhat ironic tinge. Jerry's extravagance is
not approved of. There is implied criticism in the carefully documented
description of the young man's new style of living – a move from a
single room to a three-roomed flat in a 'storied building,' the quality of
his furniture (people could see their reflections in the furniture), the
numerous suits of clothes for every occasion and the unceasing
booming of music from the mighty radiogram. All this suggests that
Jerry has already taken a false step which will bring his failure. He
refused to adhere to the sensible motto of all those struggling for
success: 'Business before Pleasure'. He is trying to have pleasure before
he has worked hard enough to deserve it. He has not even paid back his
brother's capital loan.

Jerry's fate is sealed when he falls desperately in love with Obiageli,
a pretty but heartless school-teacher who plunges him deeply into debt
and then deserts him. Before she walks out on him, she delivers this
abusive valedictory speech:

> You are bankrupt and that is why you are selling your things.
> It may interest you then to know that I don't love you any
> longer. I can't afford to marry a poor man. From today, do
> not talk to me. Of course I don't expect to see you in the bars
> of hotels [where he had lavished much of his money on her] –
> you are an idiot.

This last shot is probably the writer's opinion too. Only idiots and
suckers allow themselves to be beguiled by feckless and vulgar young
women when they have already secured the means by which they
could raise their economic position.

Apart from the full-length treatment of the economic theme, there are numerous anecdotes which bring out the authors' attitudes to the economic question. In Olisa's *Money Hard to Get But Easy To Spend* there is a cluster of anecdotes describing what happens when money seekers leave their village for the towns, what happens to those who seek 'high life' without first working for economic success, the fate of petty traders who cheat their customers, of a servant who steals his master's money and a member of a trading syndicate who cheats his co-directors, and so on. All the anecdotes show that the best way to go about earning money is the way of honest hard work. If it is praiseworthy for the individual to work hard to raise his economic position, it is even more so for him to go about it in an honest way.

The quest for happiness in the Onitsha Market literature is, in the final analysis, reduced to the quest by individuals for economic self-sufficiency and for the fruits of economic success. Education is the key which opens the door to this success. Diligence, thrift, sobriety and prudence are the cardinal virtues which continue to keep this door open. The pamphlet authors devote attention to aspects of the economic problem because by so doing they project the image of the good life, pointing the way to greater happiness and fulfilment. They regard their prescriptions as a passport to happiness.

4 Romantic Love:
Its Sources for West Africa

One of the essential points about the Onitsha Market literature is that it is rooted in contemporary life, that it tends to draw within its purview the factors which are continually shaping the attitudes and outlook of people in modern Africa. These factors impinge most strikingly on ordinary men and women whose exposure to them is relatively recent; indeed so recent that there has not been time for them to be well 'digested' and assimilated to the African experience. The consequence for the pamphlet literature as a whole has been that it reflects a certain dynamism and rawness, in the sense that characters and situations within it are in active and persistent formation. The novelty of the embodied experience is often clearly discernible.

In no other aspect of life is this more true than in the concept of romantic love. The subject is handled by many of the pamphlet authors, either as a self-contained theme or in the context of marriage. No analysis of the pamphlet literature can be complete without attention to this subject, especially to the highways and byways by which the concept has found its way into West Africa and established such a strong hold on the popular imagination.

Like the Bible, the alphabetic script, the cinema and the motor car, romantic love and the ideas associated with it, as well as the various modes of its expression, came to West Africa from the West. This is not to suggest that members of one sex did not excite others of the opposite sex in Africa or show affection for them until they learnt to do so from Western Europeans. That would be absurd and untrue. What is implied by the statement that romantic love came to Africa from the West is simply this: that the mutual attraction of people of opposite sex, and their integration through mutual affection and total preoccupation with this mutual relationship, the state which is recognized as 'being in love', receives much functional emphasis within the Western cultural tradition, and had hardly any emphasis at all within the African cultural tradition until the contact between Africa and the West altered the situation.

This is best demonstrated by example. Within a Western society no one would see anything reprehensible in a young man who is attracted strongly by a young woman taking the earliest opportunity to make contact with the object of his excitement. If the young woman in question is similarly excited, barring any serious impediments, the two people concerned might proceed to strengthen the attachment until they make intimate contact – physical, emotional, intellectual and psychological. In other words, they come to care for each other in a deeply personal way. This situation might last as long as is convenient to the parties and might then break up and the two people drift apart again. The relationship might also mature into a permanent association where both parties decide to translate the love affair into the higher level of social compact, marriage.

Certain basic cultural assumptions are at work here. First, it is accepted within the society that the attraction of people of the opposite sex is a normal human trait; secondly, that this attraction can legitimately be pursued and might lead to the formation of mutual attachment and the development of intimacies, affection and understanding; thirdly, that the society will not interfere with the association, provided that it is conducted without injury and annoyance to others; and fourthly, that the highest level of mutual integration, marriage, can and indeed should develop from this form of association.

All this is as different as can be from the situation in traditional Africa. In Africa a young man and a young woman might admire each other: this would be perfectly natural. But it would be deemed perversity for this admiration to be developed further by either or both of the individuals, or for either to attempt to establish beyond it an intimacy on his or her own initiative. The young man could certainly mobilize the support of his family to sue for the admired young woman in marriage, but personal association would be discouraged. Love attachment is out of the question for the individuals; and as for marriage, it is a compact between the families to which the married individuals belong, not an affair between the contracting individuals to which their families and well-wishers might bear witness, as in the West. The result is that whereas in the West the fate of a marriage is largely the affair of the contracting individuals, in Africa, the families of the couple are just as deeply involved.

No two systems can be more divergent in their assumptions and principles as the Western and the African systems on this matter of romantic love and marriage.

Ruth Benedict's insight into the bases of cultural variation throws some light on the matter. In her *Patterns of Culture*, she traces the behaviour of specific cultures to the principle of selection and the inter-penetration of the traits selected out of a spectrum of possibilities. She says:

> The diversity of culture results not only from the ease with which societies elaborate or reject possible aspects of existence. It is due even more to a complex interweaving of cultural traits. The final form of any [traditional] institution ... goes far beyond the original human impulse. In great measure this final form depends upon the way in which the trait has merged with other traits from different fields of experience.
>
> (*Patterns of Culture*, London, 1961, p. 26.)

The question is not whether love and sexual attraction as normal human traits exist within Western and African societies, but how they are woven into the fabric of life, how strongly they feature in the belief system, the attitudes and outlooks and the actions of individuals within the Western and African cultures.

In pre-colonial Africa, romantic love, whether as an autonomous experience or as a stepping stone to marriage, was played down and subordinated to familial and community interests. Because of the close linking of the fate of individuals to that of the group to which they belonged, a peculiarity referred to by Durkheim as 'mechanical solidarity', romantic individualism was understandably curbed by stringent taboos. For how could families go on using the institution of marriage for making desirable allies of other families if young people were free to run off and get themselves attached to anyone they took a personal fancy to? In a situation of underdevelopment and fragile political and social infra-structure, families and communities depended for stability largely on the balancing of group relationships and the linking of families and segments in marriage alliances. To give free rein to romantic love would threaten the foundations of social stability and integration.

The point made here is not peculiar to traditional African societies, but appears to apply to all pre-industrial and traditional societies. Social anthropologists like Malinowski and Margaret Mead who have studied societies widely separated from Africa have come more or less to the same conclusion. The Indian writer Chaudhuri, in his entertaining travelogue *Passage to England*, draws a sharp contrast between attitudes to love and marriage among Europeans and Indians.

Chaudhuri's study shows that Indian attitudes to love and marriage are like those of traditional Africa.

Igbo traditional society, like all pre-industrial societies, recognized marriage and child-bearing as the essential link between individuals of the opposite sex and looked with disfavour on premarital intimacy between young men and women. It insisted on chastity and virginity before marriage and marital fidelity thereafter. The earliest Igbo writer, Olaudah Equiano, bore testimony to this more than two hundred years ago, when he wrote in his autobiography:

> Our Women too were in my eyes at least uncommonly graceful, alert and modest to a degree of bashfulness; nor do I remember to have ever heard of an instance of incontinence amongst them before marriage.

(The Interesting Narrative of the Life of Olaudah Equiano, or Gustavus Vassa, the African, London, 1789.)

It can be said with a fair degree of certainty, in view of customary attitudes in Igbo society, that kissing, 'necking', hand-holding, cuddling, 'petting' and such physical expressions of romantic relationship were unknown in Igbo traditional society. Public expression of affection such as the embrace was restricted to people with close blood relationship. Several taboos, including even the prohibition of young men from stepping over the outstretched legs of young women, served in Igbo society to preserve a distance between the sexes which in turn made the realization of the basic virtue of premarital chastity possible.

In the matter of marriage, courtship was often by family intermediaries and where engaged couple had to see each other, meetings were in full view of the adult members of the boy's and girl's families. The young man who tried to procure secret meetings with the girl to whom he was engaged was soon discredited in the eyes of her family. The engagement itself might be broken off on this account. Some degree of horse-play was permitted the engaged couple, but even this had to take place in the open. The idea of romantic love for its own sake would be anathema to Igbo traditional society.

That is not to say that rustic Don Juans and forward trollops did not sometimes attempt to give the slip to custom. Indeed, as Mead has noted in the case of the Samoans, and as every Igbo society realized to its chagrin, there were cases of stolen 'encounters' and under-the-palm-tree clandestine rendezvous. But these were regarded as deviations from normal behaviour. If the culprits were unlucky enough to be discovered, they received the full weight of communal displeasure which might include their being translated into satirical songs. The vigilance of parents and other members of the extended family over growing children drastically reduced the possibility of successful flouting of the code of sexual morality.

It is often imagined, wrongly it seems, that the discipline of the traditional code of sexual morality involved the repression of individual sexual drives. There is, as far as one can see, no case of repression. Malinowski has asserted and Mead illustrated that the close control of sexual behaviour was part of a normal process of individual education in traditional society. Sexual drives were culturally and constructively directed into channels already elaborated as the people's way of life. As Ruth Benedict has put it, 'The life-history of the individual is first and foremost an accommodation to the patterns and standards traditionally handed down in his community.' Freudian psychology would have very little work for it in the context of Igbo and other traditional societies.

The contact of the West with Africa, and the introduction of Western institutions and values which stress individual experience, in contrast to those of Africa which emphasize collective tradition, have changed the situation. Western-oriented institutions provided alternatives, and an alternative set of values to which individuals could appeal. And because they represent the rising forces associated with progress and achievement, they have generally thrived at the expense of traditional institutions and values. They have tended to undermine and supplant the institutions and values of the native tradition.

Romantic love is one of the most outstanding of these newly introduced elements. Because it is essentially an individualistic experience (indeed individuals are most aggressively individualistic in love matters) romantic love exercises a strong fascination for individuals who have been exposed to the Western-oriented way of life. They find it a liberating force; once they embrace romantic love, they begin to find the old traditional way of life with its code of sexual morality too exacting and no longer tolerable. They are then most eager to absorb 'romantic' attitudes.

The concept of romantic love came to West Africans from a number of sources. The most important of these was the study of English literature in West African schools and universities. In many of the texts set for examinations, romantic attachment as a basis for marriage is vigorously promoted. Any grammar-school boy or girl who has read Shakespeare's *Romeo and Juliet, Twelfth Night* or *As You Like It,* or Jane Austen's novels, Emily Brontë's *Wuthering Heights* or even Dicken's *David Copperfield* (these are among the popular set books for English literature courses in West Africa) must be acquainted with the central position of romantic love and mutual attachment in the marriage system of the English people. These novels and plays portray romantic love as an aspect of marriage, either as their central theme or as a constant element of the background. Young people are extremely impressionable and use the experience they find in books to validate their aspirations to modernity; they cannot but be influenced by the 'romantic' notions contained in their literature texts.

The concept of romantic love is so well developed in English literature because the subject provides one of the strongest and longest-lasting veins of European civilization and has been traced by some from the earliest periods of the history of the race. Some have even associated the concept with such steadying elements in European civilization as philosophy and religion. In the view of Wallace Fowlie, in his *Love and Literature,* romantic love derived from the early development of philosophical love in classical Greece and the divine love of the Christian mystics in early Christendom. The derivation of romantic love from philosophy and religion, and the transference to human love of devotion previously paid to knowledge, to God and the Virgin have meant that the concept of love must embody a large degree of idealization, as is evident in Dante's *Divine Comedy,* and the courtly romances. The secularizing process in later periods of European history has not altogether destroyed the mystical element in the concept of love, so that a perfect union of the sexes is usually thought of in terms of a marriage of the human with the divine, the physical with the spiritual essences.

Side by side with the idealized picture of romantic love has developed the naturalistic, realistic picture which departs radically from the ideals of courtly romance, but which does not altogether obliterate it. So that even though numerous works of literature touch on the experience of physical love and explore the domain of the Don Juans, the Casanovas and the courtesans and demimondaines, the ideal embodying the spiritual and the elevated is never far from the surface. Implicit in the description of deviations from sexual norms are the norms themselves, the superstructure of values which constitute the ideal. The preservation of romantic idealism is often promoted by the habit of editors bowdlerizing school texts. They spend considerable time and effort pruning away what are considered the grosser elements from the 'romantic' notions.

But the labour spent over bowdlerized texts is wasted, for other channels were, and continue to be, available to West African readers by which to make contact with the physical aspects of romantic love. There were numerous magazines, of the family of *Woman's Own* and *True Romances,* carrying stories dealing with romantic love and marriage and going into great detail in the description of the purely physical experience of romantic love. The boy-meets-girl story which is the simplest and crudest expression of romantic love became very popular in West Africa in the 1940s. There were also romantic novels such as those of Marie Corelli and Bertha Clay which helped to shape the attitudes of those whose vision of life was being determined by new and radical influences which they had come to associate with 'the good life' and 'progress'.

The part played by Marie Corelli and Bertha Clay in advancing the spread of 'romantic' notions among the young people in West Africa deserves more attention here. One might well begin with Marie Corelli. Her books, most of which idealized romantic love and were often steeped in supernaturalism and pseudo-mysticism, were popular best sellers in Britain. She wrote a number of romances including: *The Sorrows of Satan*; *The Mighty Atom*; *A Romance of Two Worlds*; *The Soul of Lilith*; *Ziska, the Problem of a Wicked Soul*; and *Vendetta.*

The Sorrows of Satan and *Vendetta* were very popular in West Africa in the nineteen-forties and fifties, and made a great impression on the minds of young grammar school students, who read them with excitement and retailed the stories to their friends. In *The Sorrows of Satan,* for example, Marie Corelli tells how a girl who is 'pressured' by her impoverished father into marrying for money and not for love is exposed to a terrible temptation and comes to a terrible end. Such a story, with its undisguised moral comment, was sure to stiffen young West African girls in their opposition to the attempts of their fathers to impose husbands on them.

It is not far-fetched to say that such Victorian romance fiction as *The Sorrows of Satan* fulfilled the function which folk-tales fulfilled in traditional society, except that very often their didactic intentions are totally different. For example, while the romance writers used their tales to extol the virtues of marriage for love and to expose the evils of parentally arranged matches, the folk-tales, with their anti-romantic moral intentions, illustrated the dangers which beset children who try to make their own choice in marriage by flouting parental authority.

Bertha Clay was an Englishwoman whose real name was Mrs Charlotte Monica Brame. She started writing in the first decade of the twentieth century and was still writing in the 1950s. Some of her works were no bigger than pamphlets. They were bound in paper, like the Onitsha pamphlets, and sold for sixpence. Even her hard-backs cost only a few shillings. Her writing, like Marie Corelli's, dealt with romances of marriage, love, infidelity, family intrigues, and so on and included such titles as: *Another Man's Wife*; *Between Two Loves*; *Cupid's Feather*; *For Love Alone*; *In Love's Crucible*; *Love's Golden Reign*; *Love's Hidden Perils*; *The Wings of Love*; *Stolen Love*; *A Woman's Temptation*; *Wooed and Won*. Many Onitsha pamphlet titles show a close resemblance to some of these. Bertha Clay's titles are highly suggestive, and since her books cost so little, many of them became popular in West Africa among college boys and girls. They became, as it were, a school where West African adolescents made their first acquaintance with the heady notions of love. *A Woman's Temptation* was particularly popular with girls, most of whom wept bitterly as they read the sad tale of the heroine.

The point being made here is that by the nineteen forties, the average young man and woman whose education had progressed beyond the primary level had acquired enough of the 'romantic' notions of love and marriage through formal literary reading and reading of 'romantic' books and magazines to feel resentful of the old 'puritanical' code of sexual behaviour, and especially of the old custom of parentally-organized marriage.

Christianity was also an important factor making for the spread in West Africa of romantic love and the ideas associated with it. The fact is somewhat paradoxical. Christianity insists on chastity and continence, which is hardly conducive to the flowering of romantic love and attitudes. But the experience of Europe is there to show that, whether originally intended or by mere accident, Christianity has provided an allegorical frame-work for both idealized and humanized love. The perception of the divine and the enjoyment of some personal union with God by Christian mystics were expressed almost always in erotic and highly ecstatic imagery. Such images were readily pulled back into the mundane sphere and pressed into the service of romantic and carnal love. The same thing can be said of certain images built around the Church, such as that she is the 'spouse' of Christ. The church divines and mystics borrowed the images origin-ally from the physical, earthly world only to lose them later to the physical, earthly users.

But, more importantly, the insistence of Christianity on monogamy has meant that, at some stage or other, a single man would have to confront a single woman with whom he would have to forge a most individualistic and private relationship – that of the fusion of two personalities into a mystical unity. This idea is central in the teachings of the orthodox Christian sects, and much elaborate rhetoric is spent on it both by St Paul and the Evangelists. Such a concern with the relationship of one man and one woman, taken together with the imaginative development of the same concept in works of literature, romantic fiction and magazines, must necessarily deeply impress itself on the imagination of young people, among whom must be numbered the authors of the pamphlets and the audience they write for.

What has happened in Africa has been that the combined on-slaught by St Paul, St Augustine and St Ambrose, Shakespeare and Jane Austen, Marie Corelli and Bertha Clay, and those indefatigable spinners of tales about love-lorn maidens and dashing young men who dominate the 'true' romances magazines, has proved too strong for the fragile defences of the customary code of sexual morality and marriage. The result has been the emergence of romantic love as a vital factor in modern West Africa.

Nor did the matter end with mere familiarization with the abstract notions of romantic love. Its 'rituals' were eagerly learned from English literature, from boy-meets-girl romantic magazines, from romantic fiction and most dramatically, from the cinema and tele-vision. The cinema's pictorial approach has immense potential for illustrating the physical, active aspects of romantic relationship. Reading about an action is nowhere near as effective as seeing the same action enacted before one's eyes. The impact of the cinema, because the cinema concretizes experience, is more direct, emphatic and suggestive than the most skilful verbal description of the same action.

Side by side with the influence of the cinema in the introduction of the concept of romantic love in West Africa must be mentioned the part which 'love' songs played in stimulating it and supplying many of its clichés. The songs occurred originally in romantic films and were later extracted and compiled in 'record song books'. They became current in Nigeria in the 1940s and have continued to circulate ever since, elaborating and up-dating their content with the coming of new songs. Songs popularized by disc jockeys have become part of the record books without having been part of a film. Thus James Brown's 'I'm black and proud' is incorporated in the latest edition with an old favourite romantic ditty from 'Pagan Love Song'.

The first and most popular song book was issued by Chuks Bookshop of Yaba in 1947. It became one of the invaluable possessions of countless Nigerian college girls and boys in the late forties and fifties. They vied with one another as to who could sing the largest number of the hundred and more songs in the book. Love letters were full of sentiments copied directly from them, and some boys and girls went so far as to conduct their courtship and love affairs in songs taken from the record song book. The importance of the song book has relatively diminished since the 1960s, with the coming of cheap plastic records.

Romantic love, transplanted from its native Western soil onto the seemingly hostile and antipathetic soil of traditional Africa, has had such rich nourishment from an array of most disparate and incongruent nutrients that it has managed to survive in spite of the obvious odds. It has become one of the living realities of modern Africa and must therefore be taken into account by anyone who wishes to consider life on the continent and see it whole. Its existence has not been lost sight of by commentators on the state of society, least of all by the popular writers and artists who reflect the major, surface movements and appearances of the given moment. The writers of the Onitsha Market pamphlets are no exception.

5 Daughters and Fathers

Marriage is a major theme in the Onitsha Market literature. Next only to love, it engages the attention of the largest number of the popular authors. In its treatment we see one of the areas of conflict in contemporary Africa. The source of the conflict is often the determination of parents (especially fathers) to have a dominant voice in deciding who should marry their daughters, and the equally determined efforts of the daughters to resist what they regard as an intolerable interference in a matter which touches them intimately. The parents invoke the old family tradition whereby parents have a right to influence in a decisive manner their children's marriage, while their children invoke the Western marriage tradition which allows the intending couples the final say in their marriage. Most of the authors, because they belong to the generation of the children rather than that of the parents, share the view of the children in the matter, and use their medium to champion their cause and damage that of the parents. The pamphlet field is so wide, of course, that it admits of a number of significant exceptions, as we shall see.

The theme provides one of the stereotyped plots of the popular pamphlets. Usually, there is the father, the villain of the piece, who is portrayed as an old-fashioned and capricious autocrat with some private, often ignoble, motive for wishing to marry his daughter to a particular suitor whom his daughter has very good reason to abhor. The old man may show decided partiality towards this suitor because he is an old friend of the family (as in Cletus Nwosu's *Miss Cordelia in the Romance of Destiny*), because he is rich and will pay a high bride price (as in Ogali's *Veronica My Daughter*, Highbred Maxwell's *Back to Happiness* and R. Okonkwo's *The Game of Love*), because he is both rich and an old friend (as in Okenwa Olisa's *Elizabeth My Lover*), or because he is a prominent politician whose glory would be expected to reflect on his wife's family (as in Olisa's *About Husband and Wife Who Hate Themselves*).

In full confrontation with the father are the lovers, the daughter and her chosen suitor. Between these adversaries stands the mother of the family, torn between her loyalty to her husband and her maternal duty to her distressed daughter. In the end, her gentle persuasion and appeal to human compassion often triumph and she induces the father to give in to the views of the young people. After all the father is fighting for his authority, a mere abstraction when compared with the tangible fact that the daughter is fighting for her whole future and happiness.

Sociologists of the African scene put forward numerous plausible explanations for the break-down of the old marriage code in Africa and the increasing assertion by young people of Western-oriented marriage customs. One does not have to be a sociologist to see that the two principal pillars of the European domination of Africa – Christianity and modern education – transform the life-styles and alter the attitudes of present-day Africans to the extent that a number of assumptions of the old tradition are questioned or rejected. Marriage is one area of social life in which the impact of Europe is most strongly felt. The introduction of Western marriage laws as well as the inculcation of Christianity undermine the traditional system by providing an alternative to the old marriage code.

By the nineteen-forties, the average young man and woman whose education had progressed beyond the primary level had acquired enough 'romantic' notions about marriage through formal literary reading and reading 'romantic' books and magazines to begin to feel resentful of the old custom of parentally-organized marriage and to see their way out through the new dispensation.

The daughters, who suffer most when a marriage goes wrong, are therefore the most unyielding in their refusal to respect the match-making authority of their families. They are often defiant and give their reasons for flouting the views of their parents with clarity and conviction. Thus, Veronica (Ogali's *Veronica My Daughter*), a mere college girl, makes this pretty and impertinent speech to her father, rejecting his candidate and making her own choice of suitor:

> Papa, I must be candid now. I love Mike and I think nothing on earth can separate us. If you flog me, I must still love him. If you curse me, I must still love him. If you cut off my head, well, I must still love him in the world beyond. I know your opinion. You want me to marry that old illiterate man, Chief Bassey – No! the more I see him, the more I am offended. In fact, the mere sight of him is annoying: but the more I see Mike, the more I love him. I have decided to marry Mike and I assure you we are wedding in a few months time, that is a

month after the examination. If you give your hand to it – all
good. If you do not, I assure you nothing stops it.

Elizabeth in Olisa's *Elizabeth My Lover* appeals to her father thus:
Don't fight against nature. Nothing on earth stops my
marriage with Mr Ototofioko. If you like purchase ten more
guns. Whether you like it or not I must follow Ototofioko
today otherwise I die. I love Mr Ototofioko deeply and cannot
be happy without him.

Occasionally, the tone of a girl's protest is indignant, truculent or
downright abusive, as in Thomas Iguh's *Alice in the Romance of Love*
in which Alice tells her father: 'I'll paint you in the real colours that
befit a slut and octopus, a menace and a double-faced man.'

It is clear that the authors' sympathy lies with the girls, whose
attitude is regarded as 'progressive' because they stand for the
concept of marriage as an affair between two young people 'in love'
and not with the fathers who, by insisting on their customary right to
select their daughters' future husbands, are regarded as 'reactionary',
old-fashioned and a nuisance.

The authors show their support for the daughters and dislike for the
fathers in various ways. One is to make the fathers as unattractive as
possible. They are not only depicted as arbitrary, autocratic and
small-minded; they are further damned by being shown as illiterate.
The daughters and their collaborating mothers are given the virtue of
a good education and made to speak impeccable Queen's English
while the fathers speak atrocious 'pidgin'.

This is not an attested sociological fact of course; if anything, the
reverse is probably the case. Husbands were more likely, until a few
decades ago, to be literate while their wives, because women's
education was discouraged, were more likely to be illiterate, or at best,
only half-literate. The situation in the pamphlets is not a true account,
but a technique for doing down the fathers and damaging their case.

The preferred young suitors are given various kinds of excellence
which (these writers imply) qualify them incontestably for the young
girls' favour, while their rivals (the men favoured by the fathers) are
given such damnable qualities as make their aspiration appear both
ridiculous and indecent. For example, in *Veronica My Daughter,* the
favoured young suitor is not only an enterprising journalist and
'novelist' but also a holder of the inter-B.A. degree (very highly
regarded in the 1940s and 1950s) while Chief Bassey, his rival, is old,
illiterate and vulgarly rich (his idea of marriage is of something akin

to an auction sale). Again, in Benjamin Chiazor's *Back to Happiness,* the favoured suitor is an honest, hard-working student while his rival is a pretender to wealth and a thief.

This scene in *Elizabeth My Lover* brings out with dramatic force and clarity how the theme of marriage is developed, as well as the opinions of the contestants as defined by their interests and the values they invoke. It takes place in Chief Cookey's parlour, and is the crisis of the play:

> *Chief Cookey*: This thief thief boy, Ototofioko, wettin you dey find for my house? Go away quickly quickly. I go call police for you.
>
> *Ototofioko*: There is nothing bad in my coming here, Chief Cookey. May it please you to hear that I come to marry your daughter, Elizabeth.
>
> *Chief Cookey*: Bush boy, hooligan, thief thief boy and drunkard. You no go marry my daughter. You no having money I done see the big man wee go marriam. So, go, I go beatam you with my walking stick.
>
> *Cecilia (Chief Cookey's Wife)*: This is never in the least the way to treat somebody. It is offensive to refer to Ototofioko as a thief, hooligan and drunkard. He is not. Under no circumstances will you beat a person who comes to marry your daughter. Take note of this. I am in support of the marriage.
>
> *Chief Cookey*: Big woman, my master, I dey hear you. You want fighting again and you go see trouble run away. You don enter into arrangement with Ototofioko, thankio. You go see with your eyes. Ototofioko, go. I dey tell you now with clear eyes. The time we go vex, you will see paraver. I no love you, the person we I love go marry my daughter, you hear?
>
> *Elizabeth*: Papa, I wonder why you have been going astray as far as my good terms with Ototofioko is concerned. You cannot, under the fundamental human right, choose a husband for me. This is my entire right. You cannot also impose a husband on me.
>
> *Chief Cookey*: Elizabeth, I go beat you again. No talk again, Ototofioko no go marry you. Na Chief Jaja go marry you. Na my friend for long long time. He getting money plenty and go pay me £250.

Chief Jaja: I am big chief, Elizabeth, ago pay any amount
  your father charging me. This boy Ototofioko is poor. He
  no get money.

Elizabeth: Chief Jaja, my seeing you here annoys
  me. Please go with your money. If you like pay £1,000 to
  my father. You are not paying it on my head.

Chief Cookey: Chief Jaja, pay me £250 I go
  forcam marry you. Na my daughter, na me bornam. Na
  nonsense ide talk.

Cecilia: You must change with the time. This time
  is no longer the olden days when fathers forced their
  daughters to marry 'contrary to their wishes'.

Chief Cookey: Na me de control this house, whatever I decide
  na final.

Ototofioko: Chief Cookey, I cannot insult you as you have
  done to me. Be it known to you that under the law of the
  First Order you have no right to refuse my marriage with
  your daughter. You have no right also to impose a husband
  on her. So take my £30, the lawful bride price.

Chief Cookey: You are a beast, if you no go away now, I
  shoot you with my gun. Why not marry my daughter with
  1d? I no blame you. Because you never born, you no know
  the suffer we dey for burning a child. Na yim make you dey
  talk nonsense. Monkey like you.

Elizabeth: Papa, you have seriously offended me and
  Ototofioko . . . I love all the parts of his body. He is a
  gentleman of no equal, know this now or never. He has
  personality. He is handsome, healthy, cultured and
  educated. You can't beat him – unbeatable. He is my taste
  and what are you talking!

  My sweet heart, Mr. Ototofioko, is working under the
  Ministry of Communications and Aviation. He holds an
  important post but you are calling him a hooligan. Desist
  from insulting and using unbecoming words against him.
  Never mar his famous name.

Cecilia: Elizabeth my daughter, talk less, you are addressing
  your dad. My own (view) is that you can marry
  Ototofioko. He cannot compel you to marry this old,
  illiterate Chief Jaja with dirty teeth and dirty clothes. Your
  right must be respected.

> *Chief Cookey*: I am annoyed, I go fight now, every body go
> away. Ototofioko go. Misisi go, go in with your daughter. I
> dey annoyed. Chief Jaja go, tomorrow come back. You
> must marry my daughter. My word is final. Na me dey
> control this house. God forbid, woman no go control me.
> *Chief Jaja*: Okay Chief Cookey, I go come tomorrow with
> £500. Thankio Chief (Exit Chief Jaja).
> *Chief Cookey*: Ototofioko go now now. You go see trouble
> now (Chief Cookey gets hold of his big walking-stick and
> begins to flog Mr Ototofioko and Elizabeth. Mr Ototofioko
> runs away with his sweet-heart, Elizabeth. Mr Ototofioko's
> brothers also leave the parlour to go, for, Chief Cookey is
> angry).
> (Curtain falls).

The battle-lines are very clearly drawn. On one side we have the
'saints' and on the other side the 'sinners'. Elizabeth and her lover,
Ototofioko (her mother has been converted to their side) stand for the
change and modernity while Chief Cookey and his candidate, Chief
Jaja, represent tradition and conservatism. And yet this is a superficial way of looking at the episode. The issues are not as neatly
separated as might be expected in a true modernism-
versus-traditionalism conflict. At best, we have here a number of
actions and aspirations patterned largely by the immediate pressures
on those involved. The result is not the polar assertion of the values of
tradition and modernity but a selective application which suits each
individual objective. For example, Chief Cookey, who stands for the
match-making right of the family as in the traditional past, is
influenced by the pervasive materialism of the present. He wants
Chief Jaja to marry his daughter, not only because Chief Jaja is his
friend (a consideration which would not have disgraced him by
traditional standards) but also because Chief Jaja is rich and can
afford to pay the exorbitant bride price which he expects from his
daughter's marriage. This consideration is not supported by traditional authority: there was no marital custom in Igboland which put
such emphasis on the wealth of the suitor. This is pandering to
modern materialism: so Chief Cookey can be said to be motivated by
modern as well as traditional considerations. In expecting £250 for his
daughter instead of the £30 stipulated by the Eastern Nigerian
Government, Chief Cookey shows that he is both a poor traditionalist
and a bad citizen. But the author does not mean us to withdraw

sympathy from him totally. Later in the play, when we are told that
Chief Cookey also paid £250 for his wife, Cecilia, we feel a certain
sympathy for him for wanting his daughter's suitor to pay at least
what he had paid for his daughter's mother.

Cecilia supports her daughter's right to choose her own husband,
not on any principle as lofty as the 'Fundamental Human Rights'
pompously invoked by her daughter but on the simple and pragmatic
ground that people must change with the changing times. She thus
shows herself a modernist on the marriage question. But she also
shares the 'traditionalist' sentiment that children must be respectful to
their fathers, as her sharp reprimand of her daughter for unwarranted
flippancy shows.

Ototofioko, the favoured suitor, even while insisting on the new
code of marriage which allows him and Elizabeth to be the chief
actors in their own marriage drama, also acknowledges the traditional
concept of marriage as an alliance between two families rather than
the typical 'modern' concept of a contract between two individuals.
Notice that he brings his brothers with him when he approaches his
lover's family to declare his intention.

Only Elizabeth remains consistently defiant of the old and un-
swervingly committed to the present and to 'progress'. Her commitment to love as the basis of marriage is total and complete. She loves
her young man, 'all the parts of his body', and his white-collar job in
the Ministry of Communications and Aviation. Everything about
him, as seen through her lover's eyes, is perfect, and she defends his
honour and his eligibility as an aspiring husband with the courage of
complete conviction. In the end she runs off to live with him out of
wedlock when it becomes clear to her that her father will not relax his
opposition.

The episode is a good piece of domestic comedy. This is an area in
which the pamphlet authors show their competence. The situation is
explosive and charged with passion, but the writer handles it well by a
careful distribution of emphases and by drawing the characters with
consistency. Chief Cookey is consistently angry because he feels that
his right to run his household, especially his patriarchal authority over
the members of his family, is challenged by his daughter, his
daughter's lover, and most painful of all, by his wife. He feels
impotent in face of the concerted onslaught of his adversaries and this
makes him even more angry and aggressive. He can bully and
intimidate Ototofioko but, as long as the latter has his daughter's

affection and tacit support, there is very little he can do: the trump card is in other hands. His opponents have modern practice and 'civilization' to appeal to. They even have the Government on their side in the matter of how much he should be paid for his daughter. They know that their case is stronger than his, and they use their advantage with cunning and efficiency. In contrast to him, they speak fair and appear reasonable. Of course they can afford to speak fair and appear reasonable, since they are applying the pressure. Even while baiting him, they emphasize how reasonable their own conduct is, in order to show up his 'irrational' anger and unseemly violence. His wife preaches to him on how to conduct himself towards his daughter's suitors but ignores the fact that this particular suitor is unacceptable to the old man. Ototofioko draws attention to his rude behaviour and makes it clear that if he were not so well bred himself, he would pay him back in kind. And this even while doing his best to alienate the old Chief's daughter from him! To tighten the screw further, Ototofioko coolly offers to pay the legally stipulated £30, even though he knows that his rival is ready and eager to pay £500. His daughter defends her lover in words that are more likely to provoke than to conciliate. And to crown the lot, his wife declares ostentatiously that she takes her daughter's side. All this is too much for the old Chief. His reserve collapses and he reaches for his walking-stick. The episode can be seen as a successful study in malicious provocation. It is also a convincing dramatization of one of the important aspects of the marriage problem.

Some of the authors introduce refreshing variations to the theme of marriage. Their intention is equally to demonstrate that it is not advisable for parents to compel their daughters to marry people they do not love. Such marriages are shown to fail in the end, to the discomfiture of the autocratic fathers. In Okenwa Olisa's *About Husband And Wife Who Hate Themselves* the marriage is seen to be on the rocks soon after it is contracted. Husband and wife engage in a war of attrition against each other. The opening scene is a realistic portrayal of a household in disarray. The dialogue indicates the degree of antipathy which has built up between the couple. The husband has just come back from work and finds his wife sitting gloomily in a corner, doing nothing:

> *Mark*: This woman, why have you never finished the cooking by this time?
> *Victoria*: 'Z'

Mark: You say what?
Victoria: What heard you?
Mark: I heard about your head.
Victoria: You can hear about your nose.
Mark: Nonsense woman, who are you talking to?
Victoria: Nonsense man, am talking to your father.
Mark: To my father-a! to my father-a!

A fight follows, as might be expected, in which the resentful wife picks up her mortar pestle and hits her husband on the head. Neighbours and relatives are called in to arbitrate in the quarrel, and most of them agree that the marriage is an unfortunate affair which should never have taken place. They declare that Victoria's father has done wrong by forcibly marrying her to someone she did not love.

The point about this dialogue is that both husband and wife are potentially hostile because there is no love lost between them. The dialogue is a successful little study in deliberate provocation and malice. The cryptic answers of the inwardly resentful wife are calculated as an insult and defiance. Her reference to her husband's father is an extreme provocation. You can abuse a man and get away with it, but the mere mention of his father in a hostile exchange (as this one surely is) must invite violent and instant reactions from him. The husband, for his own part, is aware that his wife resents him and this makes him unduly aggressive. His reference to his wife as 'This woman' is itself a provocation worthy of the kind of answers he is given.

The point is adequately made that a marriage not based on the mutual consent of the contracting individuals is doomed to failure. The individuals will inevitably annoy and finally attack each other. In some cases, like the one between Victoria and Mark, the wretched relationship is broken up and the individuals are free to order their lives anew. In others, such as that described in Okonyia's *Tragic Niger Tales*, there is tragedy and one or other of the parties is permanently damaged by the ensuing bitterness and mutual hatred.

Naturally we have reservations about the over-generalized assumptions of the pamphlet authors on this matter of love and the marriage-relationship. They seem to have too much confidence in the all-sustaining strength of love in marriage. And this love is often built on no sounder basis than that the man involved is young, is ambitious, has attractive manners and is physically appealing. Marriage certainly needs stronger props than these, and it is immature

and unrealistic to think of marriage almost entirely in terms of love,
without at the same time considering the means of supporting the
home. Prudence dictates that the material aspect of the married state
be given its weight. The economic problems of marriage cannot be
sneered out of existence, nor can the fact that love itself is soon
fatigued if it has to be sustained by an empty belly and under the
emotional strain of a lack of the basic necessities of life.

There is an Igbo saying that what an old man sees sitting might
elude a young man even when he climbs a tree. In the matter of
determining suitability in marriage, perhaps age with its accumulation
of experience might prove helpful to the inexperience of youth.

The traditional Igbo attitude to marriage is that, given certain basic
pre-conditions such as a good family background (including the fact
that the parents are good, honest and decent people, that there is no
hereditary disease or crime in the family and that the family is not
fond of going to law), adequate material circumstances, the quality of
strength, manliness, good sense and good breeding in the young
suitor, and the full support of the adult members of the families of the
couple, there is no reason why a marriage between a man and a
woman should not prove successful. A further consideration is that
neither of the two people should have a physical revulsion for the
other. Given all these conditions, the Igbo believe that a man and a
woman could enter into marriage, and mutual accommodation and
affection will grow along with domestic intimacy. In other words,
young people are encouraged to seek first the substantial things of
marriage and 'romance' will be added unto them, not the other way
round as is constantly made out by the pamphlet authors. The older
people who advise young intending couples on the basis of the
traditional norms cannot be totally at odds with the prudential and
sensible among the young.

Often enough, older people complicate and confound the problems
of the young in the matter of marriage. Here is the real problem.
Parents with marriageable daughters, especially if they are not
well-to-do, tend to prefer suitors who are best able to pay them a high
bride price. The happiness of their daughters becomes a secondary
consideration to their desire to make money. This tendency was very
much accentuated in eastern Nigeria in the years after the end of the
second world war when many returning ex-servicemen, armed with
their considerable war bonuses, outbid all their rivals in their determination to collect the most beautiful women. Gone for ever were the

days when a man could obtain a wife by making a token payment of a few bags of cowrie shells, a few yams and livestock. With the introduction of a modern economy based on the cash nexus, a man had to pay hard cash and pay it abundantly before he could hope to procure a wife for himself. The return of the soldiers made marriage a very costly exercise, almost out of the reach of the not-very-well-to-do. School teachers, artisans, students, peasant farmers and even low-level white-collar workers suddenly found themselves stripped of their girl-friends and fiancées. Unscrupulous parents did a roaring business conferring their daughters on those who could afford to pay the highest prices. The position became scandalous as bride prices soared from under £50 before the war in many parts of eastern Nigeria to anything above £100 after the war. In fact, in some towns in Onitsha and Owerri Provinces, the bridal money for a girl who had an elementary education rose to £300.

Young men could hardly be expected to save up such large sums of money, and since they could not help getting married, many of them found themselves in the clutches of money-lenders. The Eastern Nigerian Government, in an attempt to remove the hardship caused by high bride-prices, enacted a law in 1953 restricting the bride-price to £30. In spite of legislation, however, unscrupulous fathers found a way of circumventing the provision. They issued receipts for £30 to young men who might have paid anything up to £200 or more. A thriving 'black' market went on and still goes on behind the scenes, and a prospective husband might find his would-be father-in-law suddenly turning against him if he proves too insistent on his right to pay the 'government' rather than the 'proper' price. He may actually see his girl snatched away by a wealthy old man or a prosperous polygamist who is prepared to do the 'right' thing.

The pamphlet authors belong to the low-income group which suffers most from the avarice of parents, so they glorify girls who are strong enough to defy their mercenary parents and stand up for their rights and their young unwealthy lovers. When they hand out rough treatment in their books to parents who attempt to marry their daughters against their will to wealthy suitors, these writers are dealing with a subject which, if it has not affected them personally, has probably affected some of their friends and certainly many of their readers. They handle the theme with a crusading zeal against a much-hated social abuse.

The scope of the pamphlet literature is too wide for absolute unanimity on any subject. In this matter of marriage, there are significant differences of opinion among some authors. In Momoh Aroye's *Stella at a Beauty and Fashion Parade,* Stella, a much idealized heroine, is a 'modern' girl who respects traditional values. She loves flowers and modern ballroom dancing and is fairly well-educated. And yet she marries a man chosen for her by her father and makes her family life a model for other young women to copy. In Nwosu's *Miss Cordelia in the Romance of Destiny,* Cordelia begins by rejecting a man chosen for her by her father and selecting her own young man. Just before the marriage takes place, the priestesses of the town prohibit it on the traditional ground that the couple are distantly related and so cannot become husband and wife. In Ngoh's *Florence in the River of Temptation,* Florence actually tells her lover that though she loves him and very much wishes to marry him, he must first write and obtain her father's consent. This the young man does, and since Florence's father proves reasonably agreeable, the marriage is happily celebrated.

In most of the pamphlets, young girls put love above every other consideration. But there are some exceptions. A girl may actually desert a young man to whom she is deeply attached for a more educated and a wealthier suitor who would provide her with greater economic security. Such is the theme of Egemonye's *Broken Engagement.* Here, the perfidious young lady leaves her grammar-school boy-friend and marries a U.K. trained lawyer who is also a Ph.D. The author tries to soften the blow by declaring that, 'In fact, she confessed that she loved that man and held him in honour as her Lord and husband but that her secret thoughts, were on Dammy' [the jilted young lover]. There is no doubt however that this young lady who sacrifices love to status and economic security is seen by the author as extremely perverse.

This last novelette reveals a surprising grasp of the complexity of human motives and actions. It shows that what is ideal may not always be attainable and that the best of aspirations may sometimes be thwarted by unforeseen circumstances. Such maturity in the handling of theme appears only intermittently in the pamphlet literature and shows when it does that not all the pamphlet authors are naive or innocent in their view of the contemporary life.

In addition to marriage proper, some pamphlet authors are concerned with the problem of marital infidelity and use their stories to show how it originates. Often it is shown to be the inevitable consequence of a man's injudicious choice of a wife. In N. O. Madu's *Miss Rosy in the Romance of True Love,* the unfaithful wife is a 'been-to', a girl who has been educated in the United Kingdom. Her illicit lover is an unemployed young man whom she has seduced by a mixture of bribery and allure. Later in the story, the deceived husband asserts his dignity, expels his 'been-to' wife and marries 'a big village illiterate.'

The prejudice against girls who have been educated abroad, especially in Europe and America, is one which most West African readers will recognize, because it is widely held. These girls are generally regarded as wilful, proud, 'over-sophisticated' and laden with those foreign vices which are never clearly defined but often darkly hinted at. They are therefore often regarded as unmarriageable except perhaps, by men who, like themselves, have also been educated abroad. Any 'non-been-to' aspiring to marry a 'been-to' is regarded as taking an obvious risk.

The tone in which the prejudice against 'been-to' girls is expressed is quite often high-pitched, and those who fall victim to such girls are thoroughly vilified. Such is the case of Joe in the pamphlet referred to above, when the author tells us:

> Poor Joe, whose father was remitting money monthly, fell a
> helpless prey to that perilous form of amusement namely
> smiling, talking biggishly and capering everywhere and at any
> moment with the standard enemies of progress . . . been-to
> girls.

> (N. O. Madu, *Miss Rosy in the Romance of True Love*)

As is often the case with such popular prejudices, it is difficult to separate fact from fiction. But it would be surprising if African girls, who have studied, lived or worked in highly industrialized and urbanized Europe and America, especially if they have spent many years there, were not influenced by the relatively more independent outlook of women in those parts of the world. These girls would have imbibed ideas on the place of women in modern society which their stay-at-home men and women tend to find too advanced, and to stigmatize by the term 'been-to'.

Distrust of foreign manners and influences is as old as international human intercourse. There are, for example, in Elizabethan popular pamphlets numerous satirical comments about travelled Englishmen who ape foreign manners of dress and speech, the attack being directed against the Italian modes of dress and the injection of Italian words and phrases into the English language. In West Africa the term 'been-to' expresses similar disapproval of the display of foreign manners and attitudes by West Africans who have lived abroad.

Onitsha pamphlet authors, reflecting popular prejudice, show marked dislike for 'been-to's' in their works. In their tendency to adopt extreme positions, they suggest, as in the last-mentioned work, that the antithesis of the spoilt foreign-trained woman is the unsophisticated and unspoilt village damsel.

It is hazardous, in their opinion, for a man to marry the former, and much safer to plump for the latter. This is an obvious oversimplification, since there are many 'been-to' wives who are living faithfully and happily with their husbands, marital infidelity is not unknown in the villages, nor is every illiterate country wife an angel of God. In one respect, however, the pamphlet authors may be near the truth in this matter. They could be right when they suggest that 'been-to' wives are best left to the 'been-to' husbands, who are more likely to find more common grounds of ideas and attitudes. Identity of background and experience is an important factor in the determination of successful marriages.

Some of the pamphlet authors consider the case where 'local' girls are unfaithful to their husbands. Where a man marries a girl without knowing much about her family background or after too brief a courtship, the pamphlet authors see the situation as potentially doomed to end in infidelity. Thus in Ogu's *How to Fall in Love With Girls* (a title chosen more for its sales attraction than for its bearing on the story within), the young man meets a girl at a dance and marries her soon afterwards without so much as making an effort to know her antecedents and family background. She proves unfaithful and later assaults her husband's mother, an action which discredits her utterly. In Okonkwo's *Never Trust All That Love You,* a man takes his newly married wife on a visit to his friend, and his wife there and then falls in love with the friend and begins to see him clandestinely. The marriage is later dissolved after one of those stage-managed melodramatic scenes in which the injured husband, the bride's relations and the policeman actually witness the act of infidelity. Here, the marriage fails because the couple are married, as the author is at pains to emphasize, after only a couple of months of courtship.

Marriage is an important theme in the popular pamphlets because it brings so many problems that affect individuals. The writers attempt to help to resolve some of these problems. In a rapidly changing society, with confusion of ideals and conflict of values, the popular authors feel called upon to throw some light on the main sources of the unhappiness of individuals in their aspiration to marriage, and to warn against the dangers of injudicious choice of marriage partners. Where they are not illustrating their points through fictional treatment, they write straightforward tracts containing advice and prescriptions for successful marriage. The best example of a marriage tract is Ude's *Nigerian Bachelor's Guide* which for its exhaustiveness in the treatment of the problem of marriage and its author's levelheadedness and maturity of views is yet to be equalled in the pamphlet literature.

The important fact which emerges from the treatment of marriage in the pamphlet literature is that people have freedom to choose. They may decide to follow the way of their ancestors, or they may choose to follow the modern way very much influenced by the introduced foreign institutions. Whichever way they decide to follow may determine whether they attain integration and happiness or be destroyed by pain and bitterness. The writers merely project a number of insights based on their own preconceptions as to what should be the sensible way to follow. But the choice remains for the individual.

6   The Love of Love

The theme of love genuinely excites the Onitsha Market pamphleteers. They see it in all its aspects – glorious and triumphant, tragic, comic and even melodramatic. From whatever aspect, the subject fascinates them. They revel in it and write about it with the feeling and the degree of seriousness which people display towards a newly discovered reality or a new experience. The subject is so popular that a high proportion of the creative pamphlets (perhaps up to a third) deal with it. The variety of ways in which the writers see the subject is reflected in such titles as: *The Voice of Love*; *Public Opinion on Lovers*; *Love in the Real Sense*; *Salutation is not Love*; *Love is Infallible*; *The Sorrows of Love*; *The Bitterness of Love*; *The Miracles of Love*; *Tragic Love*; *Disaster in the Realm of Love*; *They Died in the Bloom of Love*; *The Price of Love*; *The Disappointed Lover*; *Love with Tears*; *The Game of Love*; *Romance in a Nutshell*; *Love is Immortal*; *Love at First, Hate at Last*; *The Sweetness and Kingdom of Love*; *The Temple of Love,* and so on, and so forth.

For many of the young writers, it is an intoxicant which they drain with eagerness in order to give themselves a feeling of living in the present, of being 'modern' in outlook. They express extravagant, high-blown sentiments about love, often in verse or what passes for verse. Thus, a character wishing his girl-friend farewell, describes his conception of love in a lengthy verse:

> Love is the precious jewel in our life.
> The Sweetest thing this earth has ever known.
> Found in a labourer's cottage, on a stool,
> Then in a palace, sitting on a throne.
>
> (Highbred Maxwell: *Forget Me Not*)

The association of love with verse in the popular pamphlets owes everything to the study by the authors of English Literature, where so many poems deal with the theme of love. Many young lovers in the Onitsha pamphlets regard verse as the proper form for conveying their sentiments. In Adiele Madumere's *Make Friends,* for instance, two girls crossed in a love triangle compose lengthy sentimental poems telling the story of their unfortunate experience before actually

taking their own lives, thus converting a potential tragedy to melo-
drama. The verses destroy the sense of reality of the situation.

It was Tennyson who describes the poet as
        Dowered with the hate of hate, the scorn of scorn,
        The love of love . . .

The popular authors, because they take their idea of love from
poetry (often poorly digested), tend to see it in terms of stock
sentiments and express it in cliches. They are often, like the poets, in
love with the idea of being in love. Thus, a grammar school boy who
is prevented from doing his homework by his girl-friend justifies
himself by making this exaggerated speech in praise of love:

        What is a Secondary School and what is an examination?
        What do I care for the future life since the present is heaven to
        me? I cannot imagine any other temporal thing a man can
        require in this life if he got a sweetheart. Wealth? Damn it.
        Education? Forget about it. I am better off than the richest
        American filmstar or the most famous university professor
        when I have my arms around you.

When later the voice of tradition intervenes to break up this
whirl-wind love affair (unknown to themselves, the boy and the girl
are cousins) the boy writes a disappointing letter to his girl accusing
her of leading him astray. 'Deceived by the thrills of your hungry
kisses', he writes in retrospect, 'I was unable to find out whether your
love was actually a righteous one or whether it was merely an
admiration of my boyish loveliness and sportsmanship.' (Nwosu:
Miss Cordelia in the Romance of Destiny.)

There are many cases like this, which show that the authors (and
through them, their characters) have no real feeling for the true import
of romantic love. The idea alone captivates their imagination, making
them aspire to it with the single-mindedness with which they go after
everything they regard as progressive and desirable. In the same
novelette, a girl tells her friend who is somewhat late in catching the
fancy: 'I am surprised . . . that at this stage of your life you have not
even heard of the word "love". No wonder you were often sullen and
lonely.'

Love, in the pamphlets, is not always a triumphant or satisfying
experience for the young men and women who expect so much from
it. They are beginning to learn the lesson which people in Europe and
America have learnt in the hard school of experience, that ideally
satisfactory love is only found in the airy songs of French trouba-

dours or courtly romances. Translated into real human terms, into a matter of everyday relationships between real men and women, it is fraught with all sorts of hazards. Those who seek security in the love relationship alone may end by losing what security they already have. In the Onitsha popular pamphlets, there are numerous instances in which love has become a mere pretext for the exploitation of the man by the woman and vice versa. This is clearly evident in the agonized cry of this exploited lover in Highbred Maxwell's *Public Opinion on Lovers:*

> Love is a walking shadow
> Maria has deserted me
> All I spend no refund
> Rice and beans all I cooked
> Meat and bread, butter and milk
> Coffee and tea now and then
> Theatre with taxi all I paid
> Cloth or powder all my expense
> Come and go transport I paid
> Business I left for Maria's sake
> Legal action will pay the debt.

It is doubtful whether the last hope would be fulfilled. If concern with love has a lesson for the individual, it is that love's 'sweet' consequences must be taken with the 'bitter'.

Exploitation of individuals by those they are in love with is so commonplace that the pamphlet authors use their works to warn their readers against the danger. The principal danger they warn against is material exploitation. Men as well as women are shown as capable of exploiting the opposite sex in the name of love, though there are more stories of women exploiters in the pamphlets.

Prostitutes and 'free' women who live by exploiting the love propensity of the men are an obvious target. The most sustained warning against them is contained in Olisa's *Why Harlots Love Bachelors and Hate Married Men*. It reads in part:

> Why harlots, independent women, mostly lip-painted ladies, love bachelors is because they know that bachelors have a long way to go with them, they will have to see them, and also will have to take care of their pride. They come to remember what they use to get from them to buy their needs such as rekyi-rekyi, popo-cloth, velvet, ejecombe Lawyer, sasarobia scent, fine pomade, gold and silver, headtie, handkerchiefs,

> Umbrella, shoes, skirt and blouse, sandals, iron beds,
> blankets, bedsheets, pillows and pillow-cases, sleeping gowns,
> cushion chairs and covers, door blinds, window blinds,
> mosquito nets, tables and table-cloths, carpets, bed curtains,
> ladies' watches, looking glass, powder, ladies' sewing
> machines, portmanteaux, trunk box, bicycle, gramophone and
> so many other things a woman could use.

This list shows the practical interest, the attention to detail, already noticed in the section on money and material possessions. But the idea that women who want money and material things from love prefer bachelors to married men is contestable. Women out to exploit men financially and materially tend to prefer married men for at least two reasons. Married men usually have more money than young unmarried men; and in a relationship between a 'free' woman and a married man, the economic basis is often beyond question, whereas a bachelor, by dangling the prospect of marriage as bait to the single woman, might escape paying the material cost of sustaining the relationship. But bachelors (like the one so ruthlessly exploited by Maria) may be as much the victims of female exploitation as married men.

Men are shown also as exploiters. Here, for example, is the story of an exploited girl, told to her friend, in J. O. Nnadozie's *What Women Are Thinking About Men:*

> I used to buy clothes for some of my male friends and spend
> for them at such rate that only a sister can do for a brother.
> My reward afterwards was nothing but fighting, quarrelling
> and damnation. One of them whom I very much loved told me
> one day that he didn't love me again. He continued: 'Do not
> come to my house again, bloody fool!' I thought that he might
> have some defect in his brain. At any rate, I came to discover
> that he was quite normal. Earlier, he had promised me
> marriage.

The lesson that love can become an excuse for exploitation has made young people cautious in their relationships. They regard love as a game of wits in which the most trusting is soon brought low. The pamphlet authors therefore put their readers on their guard. They show girls and boys acting as confidants and advisers to one another on the matter of falling in and out of love. This dialogue in R. Okonkwo's *Why Boys Never Trust Money-Monger Girls* suggests the kind of advice one girl may give to another against being too trusting in love:

Cordelia: Friend, you have turned a new chapter in my life.
You have made me to remember the words of one Lady
Maxwell, an English Author, who once said that 'girls
without boy friends will never be happy'. But I am afraid
because to make friends with boys of the present time is
delicate.

Comfort: To make friends with boys may be delicate if one
does not know the method and tricks to follow them.

Cordelia: Please teach me the method and tricks, I beg you.

Comfort: Love your friend but do not trust him immediately
you fall in love with him. Pretend in his presence as if to
say that you have not got any other boy-friend except him.
Always tell him that you love him, for this will help you to
get many things from him. Secondly, do not be visiting
your boy-friends in the night for this can put you into
temptation. You know that boys of nowadays can't be fully
trusted. When he gets you and puts you in a motherly
condition, he will sack you and make you his enemy.

We may deplore Comfort's advice to her friend, which seems a
travesty of the spirit of romantic love, but we cannot doubt that its
cold-blooded cynicism is some kind of an attempt at meeting a real
problem. Girls are the more likely to suffer when relationships go
wrong, and they need some help to cope with 'boys of nowadays'.
That last phrase about boys making them into enemies after putting
them 'in a motherly condition' strikes a realistic note.

Some of the pamphleteers warn young girls of the danger of
becoming unmarried mothers if they do not use caution in their love
relationships. This is the theme of Gilbert Nwankwo's *Tragic Love
and the Woman from Nowhere*. In this story, when the young girl
discovers that she is expecting her lover's baby, she goes to seek
comfort from him in the town where he works. The young man runs
away from his lodgings leaving behind a piece of paper containing
this brief letter:

Dear Agnes,
I received your letter and was frightened. I cannot possibly
marry you now. I have no money.
We have made a grave mistake and must part. Forget me and
forgive.   Yours, C.

The young girl cannot now go home to face her parents' anger and disappointment, and she drifts alone into the hostile world. Nwankwo adds, superfluously: 'And so one young life had been sacrificed on the altar of love.'

This keynote is widely heard in the love pamphlets. For example, in Thomas Iguh's *The Sorrows of Love,* the chief character, an ordinary school boy, wastes his time running from one girl to another until a triangle develops, leading to an eruption of violence. The young philanderer is killed by two of his girl friends.

Like the other themes of the pamphlet literature, the writers see love in black-and-white terms. The believers write their stories showing what a marvellous experience it can be, to show that it is long suffering, trustful and beautiful. The sceptics try to prove that it is none of those things, but leads to exploitation, material and emotional, loss of security and very often death. We may relate this tendency towards rigidly simple views to the didactic impulse of the writing. In spite of their extreme positions, however, the authors' portrayal of love is often convincing because of its potential truth to life.

Some pamphlet authors regard the pursuit of love as an art, with a certain mystique, and requiring, for success, the application of the right approach and techniques. They believe that these can be successfully taught. They therefore produce works to teach others the art and technique of love. Such works bear titles like: *How to Speak To Girls and Win Their Love*; *How to Speak and Write to Girls for Friendship*; *The Way To Make Friends With Girls*; *How to Get a Lady in Love and Romance With Her*; *The Art of Love in the Real Sense.* One of the most prolific producers of advice on love, Felix N. Stephen, has written, among other works; *The School of Love and How to Attend It*; *A Journey into Love*; *How to Play Love*; *How to Get a Lady in Love.*

Some of these pamphlets advise their readers to be prudent in their love relationships; they particularly stress that it is dangerous for those in love to be precipitate in their responses. It would be sensible sometimes to test the seriousness of the other party by feigning indifference, by an abrupt cessation of correspondence or by withholding gifts. Would-be lovers are sometimes advised not to write too frequently or too promptly to avoid being taken too easily for granted.

In this matter of inculcating the right approach to the art of love, much is made of love-letters. Many of the pamphlets purport to teach the reader how to compose love-letters. They carry such titles as: *How to Write Love Letters*; *95 Love Letters and How to Compose Them*; *Our Modern Love Letters*.

The composers of model love-letters attempt to cover all occasions and to meet all exigencies. There are letters soliciting marriage, letters turning down marriage proposals, letters requesting a girl's or a boy's love, letters rejecting love, letters expressing plain admiration, letters seeking simple friendship, letters breaking off an engagement or calling off a love affair, letters making appointments or refusing them.

These letters are often outspoken, confessing feelings which are normally concealed or disguised. Where in an actual love encounter the moves and counter moves might develop into elaborate shadow boxing, the love-letter is endearingly direct and uncomplicated, as in the following engagement letters from J. Abiakam's *How to Write and Reply Letters for Marriage, Engagement Letters, Love Letters* ... The first letter is from a boy to a girl:

> No. 5 Ikoba Road,
> Benin City.

> No. 6 Riluko Road,
> Benin City.
> Dear Anti,
> I can no longer endure to tell you the opinion I have of you. I since decided to engage you but I found it difficult to contact you directly. I idiomatically mentioned of it to you during our last social gathering but I found out that you did not understand me. Therefore I put it in writing and hope to get your reply as early as possible.
> You know very well how girls chase me yet I decided to adhere to you.
> Wishing you God's blessing.

> Yours truly, J. P. Otobo.

To which Anti sends the following reply:

> No. 6 Riluko Road,
> Benin City.

> No. 5 Ikoba Road,
> Benin City.
> Sir,
> Your letter of engagement reached me recently. I thank you very much.

Indeed I have adequate love in you and I wish to grant
your request but I entertain fear for one reason. Many boys
have made it their occupation to disappoint girls. I have a
friend named Veronica. She was engaged to a young man who
used her as an instrument of his happiness but eventually he
disappointed her. Many girls have been put in a family way in
pretence of marriage which did never materialize. Therefore
my consent is subject to your honesty.

I am, Yours honest intended, A. U. Odiboli.

It is not only the young men who seek engagement with desirable
young women by writing to them. Sometimes, a girl undertakes to
write and propose, and may follow up with a threat to end the
existing association unless her young man goes through a formal
ceremony. Such is the letter from Ifeyinwa to Eric which reads as
follows:

Dear Eric,
Why is it that I have not heard from you since a month or so?
I know you will try to escape my blame by claiming that your
long silence is due to the pressure of time. Really your work is
not a small one and you are always tired whenever you come
back from school but this is not reason why you should keep
[me] in suspense of information about life in Onitsha which I
know is always cadden with terrifying news.

Well, Eric, you know fully well that it has taken a long time
since we began our friendship. After taking this fact into a
constructive consideration, I found that we must either be one
now by being married or separate. I am putting this to you
having much consideration on my age which is nearing 21.
This is a marriageable girl and it is sheer folly for me to
continue to deceive myself by indulging in friendship without
being truly engaged. Choose now or never for I am serious
about it.

Till you reply, greetings to all.

I am, Your lovely, Ife.

Eric replies, full of gratitude to be saved from an awkward
situation:

Having read with keenest understanding and avid interest
your meaningfully worded letter, I now think it opportune
and indeed mannerly to reply [to] it. Frankly speaking, I
never knew that you had the same feeling I have for you

for me. Thank you very much for this for I must cherish
your oneness of mine soon.

I will not hesitate to (let) you know that I have really
compromised to engage you for the same genuine thought (had)
been lingering in my mind but I was fearing that you would
not accept it at present. I will be yours till the last great day
when it may please our Creator to call any of us to the realm
of the past men, who of course may have enjoyed his kingdom
according to their individual stewardship on earth.

Normally we will have to exchange rings as a way of
indicating our real and legitimate promise.

These model letters might be expected to be stereotyped and
unrealistic simply because they are designed to deal with stereotyped
situations and express stock sentiments. But this is often not the case.
The letters create their own situations, and heighten credibility by
introducing circumstantial details to suit each particular context.
Their authors have a sense of the individuals who are supposed to be
writing. In a modest way, each letter expresses a different personality
and builds up its own situation. If we compare the two pairs of
characters expressed in the letters above, the differences stand out.
Otobo, who reminds the girl he wants to marry that he is sought after
by many girls, is a different character type from Eric who is too shy
to speak out. The one is almost conferring a favour, while the other is
grateful that he is thought worthy. Similarly, it is obvious that Anti
who will consent to an engagement provided her lover is on his best
behaviour, is a different character from Ifeyinwa who issues an
ultimatum to her boy to become engaged to her 'now or never'.

The variation in language also relieves the letters of monotomy.
Each of the four letters has some point of interest which is not entirely
a result of change in circumstantial details but a result of a felicitous
turn of language. For instance, Otobo's unsuccessful attempt to
convey his intention to Anti is put thus interestingly:

I idiomatically mentioned of it to you . . .

The use of 'idiomatically' here is novel and surprisingly apt. Again,
when Anti says that 'Many boys have made it their occupation to
disappoint girls' one has the impression that she is exaggerating, and
yet the word 'occupation' is oddly suitable. The long and round-about
way in which Eric expresses the separation by death of a married
couple is a fine example of the language-play which is one of the most
fascinating features of the pamphlet literature:

> I will be yours till the last great day when it may please our
> Creator to call any of us to the realm of the past men, who of
> course may have enjoyed his kingdom according to their
> individual stewardship on earth.

This is certainly a more picturesque way of putting it than to say
simply: 'I will be yours till death do us part'. Eric's 'realm of past men'
seems to represent a peculiar admixture of the ancestral and the
Christian heaven.

The model letters have an interest in their own right as a result of
these features. Though they are meant to be used by those who copy
them to meet their amatory needs, they are more often than not read
for the entertainment they provide, as well as for the shrewd insights
into romantic love and the marriage aspirations of young people.

The device of letter-writing in love affairs is convenient to the
young lovers, especially to those of them who are too shy (and it
seems many of them are) to express their love face-to-face. Where
parents are hostile to a relationship, letters are an ideal way of
carrying on a clandestine relationship and eluding detection. In some
cases, the use of a letter to state a specific proposal may be the writer's
way of giving weight to what he has to say and of underlining its
importance. In this category is obviously this letter written by the
young man to his girl-friend in Chike Okonyia's *The Tragic Niger
Tales.*

> The Idol of my Heart,
> I am seizing this opportunity to let you know that I have
> succeeded at last in convincing my daddy over that our
> marriage problem. Nothing is now in our way and from now
> on let us suppose that it will all be plain-sailing.
>   When we meet this evening, we shall be able to discuss our
> future plans.
>   Meanwhile I remain, Yours, always and ever, Byron.

Byron is writing to a girl who lives in the neighbourhood, but like
many young men of his age – the new initiates to the art of love – the
love-letter is a way of pouring out the heart in a kind of abstracted
profusion where the actual presence of the object of his love might
undermine self-confidence and inhibit eloquence.

Sometimes the letter is an admirable medium for unburdening the
oppressed heart. Characters in the popular pamphlets have now and
again to confront painful implications of broken love affairs. Where a
face-to-face encounter would make the pain of dissolution unbearable,

the letter provides a vicarious remove which reduces distress, objecti-
fies disappointment and minimizes the shock of separation. Such is
the function of this letter from an engaged young man to his
perfidious fiancée who has defected to his friend:

Rosy mine,

I am projecting this missive under a stormy frame of mind.
Within the last two days many things have happened to the
effect that I cannot help doubting your sincerity to me. It is
unnecessary here to trace back how we had started over a
year ago. But, in the pilgrimage of life two words seem to be
playing dominant part in the fields of human relation, and
they are 'Yes' and 'No'.

Now, if on the day we met you had flung a sparkling 'No'
at me over my request, I need not complain now. Besides, I
did not hide anything about me – to you. That I am poor is no
longer a news. You know it even better than I do. If it is
a crime, I am happy that not myself alone; but almost
ninety percent of the human race will pay the penalty. I
cannot remember how many rich people I have met since
morning.

Something is perhaps wrong somewhere hence I have no
doubt that you have fallen prey to momentous emotion. But
whatever happens, it was G. K. C. who wrote the following
lucid lines: 'True love has ten thousand griefs, impatiences
and resentments, that render a man unamiable in the eyes of a
person whose affection he solicits; besides that, it sinks his
figure, gives him fears and apprehensions and poorness of
spirit; and often makes him appear ridiculous where he has a
mind to recommend himself.' This is just my position before
you. You may look down on me now but you cannot
successfully look down on my future.

Meanwhile, I am assuring you that even though your
present behaviour has a tremendous impact upon both my
mental and physical set-up; nevertheless, we are not going to
be enemies. You can go anywhere you please. For it was Sir
Robert Peel who said: 'We can go forward; we can go
backward, but we cannot stand still.' And when the immortal
Mahatma Ghandi said: 'The human race is guilty of countless
crimes I for one have special excuse for mankind; after all,
this world is not well adapted to developing good good (*sic*)',

he (Ghandi) was referring to a case of this nature in which I am a helpless victim.

Finally, as you insist on going to Aba tomorrow, (to be more precise – going with Emman) I shall come to say goodbye to you. You need not doubt my sincerity here. For I have always been sincere to you. If I fail at times; it means am humanly incapable of evincing greater sincerity.

All the best, I am, Your threatened Angel, Osmond.
(Okwudili Orizu: *The Joy of Life and Its Merriments,* pp. 29–30).

This long letter well represents one aspect of the use of letters in the pamphlet literature. The personal, emotional aspect of the situation is there in the letter but as it goes on, one becomes aware that it is giving place to the objective – intellectual. The letter-writer seems to stand away from the object that excites him, in order to see it with detachment. He indicates what he, the injured party is going through, but also attempts to find justifications for her, the inflicter of injury. There is blame, but it is not pressed hard, since everything is philosophically explained. G. K. Chesterton, Robert Peel and Mahatma Ghandi are pressed into service to this end.

This lack of hysteria and extreme personal grief, this preservation of objectivity and sense of proportion, this philosophical attitude and near stoical resignation to personal disappointment in the affairs of the heart, all help to stem the tendency of failure in the love relationship to lead to tragedy. A good many of the pamphlet authors show love as just one of the numerous problems of life, and the failure of a love relationship as just one of the many disappointments of life. This intellectualization of love and its problems relieves the subject of much of the neurosis and attendant tragedy which one encounters in Western literature.

The popular authors often associate love with marriage, and their characters no sooner find a girl or boy they are attracted to than they begin to contemplate matrimony. Jane Austen had observed that:

A lady's imagination is very rapid; it jumps from admiration to love, from love to matrimony in a moment.

(Pride and Prejudice)

In the pamphlet literature, it is not only the imagination of young women but also of young men which leaps from admiration to matrimony. Often, the young men want their girls to go through an engagement ceremony with them as a means of establishing a proprietary hold upon them. Such, obviously, is the import of this letter from a young man to his girl friend: 'I love to buy you a ring now, so that people know that you are mine. Will you allow me to do that? For your information ring will mean that we are engaged which is a thing I devoutly desire. In fact it would bring us nearer to our marriage. Think of the joy of it all, darling.'

But marriage does not always follow love in the pamphlet litera-ture, any more than in life. Nor is this surprising since to the pamphlet authors and their characters love is sometimes regarded as a game played between boys and girls at a time when they are not yet ready for marriage. It is a preparation for the actual business of living, a kind of apprenticeship for adult life. In Ugochukwu Ajokuh's *The Chains of Love* (which deals with the escapades of young grammar school boys and girls on holiday), the author describes how as the holiday draws to a close the boys strive the more frantically to find girl-friends with whom they will carry on an exchange of love-letters before the next holiday period comes round. The numerous student associations, tribal and denominational, provide an ideal meeting-ground for boys and girls during the holidays. In Igboland (as elsewhere in Nigeria) almost every town or large village has a students union and some of the Christian denominations encourage their members to form student associations. Friendships started at these associations occasionally lead to marriage when the people concerned have left school, but very often they fizzle out after a more or less lengthy exchange of sentiment-soaked love letters. As the individuals grow into maturity, they begin to take life more seriously and to outgrow the 'silly' stage of the love-letter. They come to discover the gulf separating the set sentiments of the love-poem and romance fiction from the realities of the adult relationship.

The popular authors have, in a great majority of cases, accepted romantic love and the Western concept of marriage. Romantic love and marriage are the channels through which present-day West Africans express and emphasize their individuality and their libera-tion from traditional constraint and the customary impositions of the older generation. The emergent values they espouse centre on indi-vidual responsibility. The individual man or woman, they imply, has a right of free choice in love and marriage and should abide by the consequences of his choice.

There are questions which one must ask about the pamphlet authors' projection of modern values in love and marriage. First, have the Western concepts of love, courtship and marriage been fully understood and assimilated by the people for whom they write? Second, is it wise for present-day Africans to throw overboard the values of their traditional culture, which have sustained their peoples' attitudes to love, sex and marriage from time immemorial? Are those values irrational, or inadequate to sustain a modern way of life? Which values, European or traditional-African, are capable of ensuring greater happiness for individuals, in the light of what we know about love and marriage today?

These questions are pertinent because they seem to be lost sight of or ignored by most of the pamphlet authors. In the matter of romantic love, it seems not to occur to the authors that the insistence on pre-marital chastity by most, if not all, traditional West African societies is a value to be maintained in the face of the problem of young girls put in the 'motherly condition' by the young men with whom they are 'in love'. It is not adequately considered by the popular authors that in throwing off the inconvenient but protective authority of parents, young men and women have succeeded in exposing themselves to risks at a time when, because of their limited experience of life, they are most vulnerable to the consequences.

Again, the popular authors tend to accept the outward aspects of Western romantic love and marriage while being only scantily sensitive to the underlying spirit. They know about the gestures, the holding of hands, the kiss, the passionate embrace, the grimaces, everything that attracts the one sex physically to the other. These are easily learnt from romantic fiction and from the cinema and television. But what about the tenderness, the constant effort to behave well in the presence of one's lover, the desire to please and protect the loved one? These are not as easily accessible as the external expressions of love. And yet they are the true stuff of romantic love as conceived in Europe.

In the historical memory of European people, there is the image of a brave young knight kneeling solemnly, not before the altar of God, but before a beautiful, white-bosomed maiden, his mistress, in defence of whose honour he would attempt the impossible and hazard his life. Centuries after the age of chivalry, the European male's attitude to the female sex continues to be conditioned by the ideas of chivalric romance surviving in the historic memory of the race. Every European male is a kind of a 'knight', every European female, a 'lady'. The European 'knight' gets up when the European 'lady' enters a room, he vacates a seat for her and will come to her aid when it becomes clear that the European 'lady' is in difficulty or in distress. Few European males live up to the standard but those who do not, know that they are falling short. The attitude of service, the ideal of self-abnegation which can survive the old ideals of reverence, devotion, worship and tenderness, is carried into the area of romantic love. It can give love a semi-ritual significance and make it the stepping stone to matrimony and integration.

In the African system, every male is also a 'knight'. He appreciates the admiration of the female, but he will perform feats to earn the admiration of the whole people. His motive force is not the desire to earn the love of one woman but to be worthy of the affection and respect of the whole people. When he has achieved this, any woman will be proud to share his glory, as his wife. Whereas the European 'knight' having won the admiration of his 'lady', goes to her for reward through love and marriage, the African 'knight' is endowed with a 'lady' by the community in recognition of his justification of his manhood. What he does with this 'lady' thereafter remains of serious public concern. Whereas the European man and woman seek integration and fusion of individualities in love and marriage, their African counterparts seek complementarity: whereas the European couple attempt to become one body and one flesh (to use a Christian image), the African couple remain collaborative individuals whose autonomy is attested to and constantly reinforced by the community of their fellows.

In the light of the differences in cultural conditioning, it is easy to see why in the pamphlet literature the attempt by individuals with their African background to express in European style their romantic love, falls far short of the ideal and appears somewhat ridiculous. The pamphlet authors' commitment to 'modernity' in this matter of love needs serious reconsideration.

A major influence on the Onitsha pamphlet literature is the school study of English literature by the authors. This influence is expressed in a number of ways, ranging from simple allusion to a clear imitation of titles and content of literary texts. A title like *Tribius and Folida* (Uzoh), for example, is obviously based on Shakespeare's *Troilus and Cressida*. As for literary allusions and direct quotations, they are so numerous that only a few can be referred to here.

In Thomas Iguh's *Agnes the Faithful Lover,* a girl whose father has refused her permission to marry the young man of her choice threatens to kill herself adding, 'Then my name will go into history as having died like Juliet for the cause of true love.' In *Alice in the Romance of Love,* Iguh goes further than mere allusion to *Romeo and Juliet* and patterns a whole scene very closely on Act II, Scene II of the play. Here is the parting scene after a midnight meeting between the boy and the girl. It takes place in the girl's home:

Alice: It is alright; good night. (Fidelis leaves).

Alice: Come back darling, for I can't afford to let you go without a kiss (She kisses him again).

Fidelis: Sweet heart, I shall be here again to see you tomorrow.

Alice: Is tomorrow not too far? Oh! don't you know I find it difficult to control my sentimental emotions when I don't see you for a single hour.

Fidelis: Alright darling, but for the memory of this great night, have this ring and wear it always on your finger.

Alice: In fact, I have now agreed you love me and that being the case, always count me first among those that love you dearly, for I don't think anybody loves you more than myself. Oh Sweet heart hurry out for my dad is coming.

Fidelis: Alright, goodnight. (He leaves).

Alice: Don't go please without a kiss, for it is one of the pleasures of being in love with someone of the opposite sex. (They kiss themselves again.)

Fidelis: Alright, I shall continue to remember you till we see again. (Exit Fidelis).

Alice: Oh this boy is really sweet. I don't know why I have within a short space of time loved him so much. He is my Morning Star and has ultimately stolen my heart away. No I must call him back. (She goes to the window).

Alice: Fidelis! Fidelis! Fidelis! Sweetheart (she shouts for him). Oh! you are gone far, but how do I stay alone without you. Can't you listen and answer my call? I am Alice calling you. (At this stage she turns back). He has gone far. Oh! he doesn't hear me (she cries).

There are some refreshing innovations here, such as when Alice bursts into tears where Juliet would have said a less demonstrative 'Parting is such sweet sorrow'. One interesting variation is that Iguh has sensibly chosen a dispute over a piece of land as the cause of the feud between his Igbo rural Capulets and Montagues. Even while imitating the classics, the authors do not altogether lose sight of social and environmental facts.

Shakespeare is the principal author from whom popular pamphlet writers take their allusions, plots and occasionally, titles, for two main reasons. First, he is the only English author who is always included in the literature syllabus for West African examinations. All those who offer English Literature must compulsorily 'do' a Shakespeare play. This means that it is hard to go through a full grammar school or equivalent course of education without familiarity with a number of Shakespeare's plays. By the end of a five-year grammar-school course, the literature student (and most students in West Africa offer English literature) may have studied the most popular Shakespeare school texts – *Julius Caesar, Hamlet, Macbeth, The Merchant of Venice, Romeo and Juliet, As You Like It* and perhaps *Twelfth Night*. The more enterprising read more Shakespeare than is offered for examinations.

The second reason for the popularity of Shakespeare in West Africa is that he is so memorable. Whether in such splendid set pieces as Mark Anthony's funeral oration, cryptic meaning-laden expressions like 'Life's but a walking Shadow', or swash-buckling nonsense expressions like 'I'll tickle your catastrophe', Shakespeare gives West Africans whose ears have been prepared by oral tradition to absorb rhetorical, epigrammatical and metaphorical (and highly image-laden) language an inexhaustible mine of language and thought. The writers of the popular pamphlets find it natural to quote Shakespeare's brief, pithy statements which embody little gems of human experience in support of their opinions and attitudes in much the same way as they use traditional proverbs.

The linguistic habit of using fixed expressions as a means of illustrating a statement or elaborating an idea is highly developed in West Africa. The pamphlet authors themselves are conscious of this, as is evident from the number of works recording these expressions and making them available to readers. We have among them J. Abiakam's *49 Wise Sayings, 72 Idioms, 44 Questions and Answers and Some Speeches of World Leaders, Past and Present*, N. O. Njoku's *Teach Yourself Proverbs, Idioms, Wise Sayings, Laws, Rights of a Citizen, English, Applications and Many Other Things for Schools and Colleges*, and Charles N. Eze's *Learn To Speak 360 Interesting Proverbs and Know Your True Brother*. To the pamphlet authors, to quote from Shakespeare is to be faithful to one of the persistent and instinctive linguistic realities in West Africa.

The authors are most 'Shakespearean' in their plays. For example, Ogali A. Ogali's *Mr. Rabbit is Dead* is a Shakespearean medley with strong echoes of *Julius Caesar, Hamlet* and *The Merchant of Venice*. The Congo dramas are equally rich in Shakespearean suggestion, with *Julius Caesar* and *Hamlet* again offering the closest analogies. These and other works by Shakespeare are also plundered for quotations (and mis-quotations) by the pamphlet dramatists.

Thus, in *The Last Days of Lumumba* by Thomas Iguh, Lumumba is made to harangue his apathetic countrymen against Belgian colonial rule with: 'So, good country men, I don't know what you think within yourselves but for me it is battle from now on . . .' which recalls Brutus' speech in *Julius Caesar* rousing the conspirators to move against Caesar. Elsewhere, when Belgian officers arrest Lumumba and tell him to put up his hands, like Shylock in *Merchant of Venice,* he retorts:

'On what compulsion must I! tell me.' Lumumba's companion, Mr Mpolo, exasperated by Belgian harrassment says, borrowing from Mark Anthony in his funeral oration, 'We are no stones but men.' During the trial of the Congolese nationalists, the Defence Counsel attempts to mollify the Belgian judge by quoting Portia's memorable plea to Shylock: 'The Quality of Mercy is not strained . . .' In the hour of defeat, disgrace and agony, the mind feels for an apt Shakespearean anchor and the second of Lumumba's companions, Mr Okito, remembering Cardinal Wolsey in a similar situation of defeat and despair cries out 'This is the state of man, Today he puts on the tender leaves of hope . . .'

The important thing about these quotations is that they appear in areas of great emotional tension and at crisis points in a play. Groping for an adequate language to bear the burden of such tensions and express such crises yields the richest harvest of Shakespearean allusions.

The writers also quote occasionally from authors other than Shakespeare. In *Veronica My Daughter,* for example, the hero reads a lengthy, quotation-cluttered essay titled 'Man Is a Jealous Being'. He draws his quotations from Richard Whately, Bishop Hugh Latimer, Shakespeare, G. A. Gallock, Rudyard Kipling, Benjamin Harrison, Ernest Henley and Henry Longfellow. At the end of his reading his girl friend, the patient victim on whom he inflicts the torrent of his declamation, is overwhelmed and manages to say, timidly, 'Masterpiece! How sweet! You wrote this? No wonder you are a novelist and Newspaper Columnist' – hardly an adequate response to the high-voltage stuff just poured out. Later, the same character, before a large audience of illiterates and semi-literates, makes a long, self-congratulatory speech which he clinches with eleven lines of Goethe, to the supreme edification of his audience.

The display of literary learning by the popular authors tends to destroy in some of the writing the sense of reality which they easily create in their unpretentious moments. It appears that they imagine that by inserting quotations from learned authors within their works they enhance their standing with the reader. They use the quotations to support their own opinions. To introduce or clinch a statement with a quotation from Shakespeare or Goethe or Bertha Clay gives the comfortable feeling of having protected this statement with their authority and thus rendering it unassailable save to the most vulgar intellect.

Popular authors are not alone in this. The intellectual authors sometimes indulge their love of English literature by creating situations in which their characters discuss favourite writers and their works. There is a good example of this in *No Longer at Ease,* where Achebe skilfully grafts in a brief but lucid discussion of Graham Greene's *The Heart of the Matter* and Evelyn Waugh's *A Handful of Dust.* Onuorah Nzekwu's characters in *Wand of Noble Wood* are fond of interlacing their conversation with brief discussions of literary questions. William Conton's hero in *The African* is a student of English Literature and a great enthusiast for the English classics. He uses any favourable opportunity to make this clear, either by quoting from well-known authors or comparing real people and situations to those in works of literature. We are told, for instance, that before he goes down from the grammar school, the hero and his friend spend the last night declaiming *Macbeth* to each other, that Norman architecture in Durham is 'a thing of beauty' and 'a joy for ever' and that a genial, plump, red-faced English lorry driver conjures up for the hero the picture of Mr Pickwick. The main difference between the use of literary references by the intellectual authors and by the popular ones is principally that in the works of the latter the allusions are not always well integrated into the contexts.

Related to the predilection for quoting from Shakespeare and the other English classics is the fascination with words. Nor are the pamphlet authors alone in this. English words had a great fascination for the early literate West Africans; if we go back to written works produced in the nineteenth century, we are struck by their markedly orotund style and their substitution of flamboyance of language for concreteness of thought. The polysyllabic word was then preferred to the monosyllabic one, an abstract word to a concrete one, and a long complex sentence to a simple construction.

The Black intelligentsia of the coastal towns who cultivated this ornate, elaborately woven style flourished from the second half of the nineteenth until the early decades of the twentieth century. Today, we are overcome by the great length of their sentences. They wrote so differently from us! We must, however, admire their dexterity in balancing the different parts of the long sentence and the overall effect of good workmanship and grandeur their style produces.

From the nineteen-thirties onwards, a marked decline in the quality of prose occurred. One reason might be that the change occurred as a result of the influence of America-trained journalists and professionals on the intellectual environment. (The return from America and the change coincided.) Their introduction of what one might call an automatic method of writing and the habit of slogan-making and thinking in cliches damaged the evolution of a serviceable prose style. Interest in words survived, but in place of the cleverly patterned, almost architectonic, prose of the Black Victorians (as the coastal intelligentsia came to be known), we have the formless, rambling prose of the slogan-and-cliches period of the thirties, forties and the fifties. Expressions such as 'horizontal education', 'political irredentism', 'boycott the boycottables', 'sine qua non', 'man should not be a wolf to man', 'operation bull-dozer', to take only a few, came into vogue and were often 'wedged' into already inelegant and rambling prose.

This can easily be illustrated by taking two typical passages, one representing the best example of prose stylization of the late nineteenth century, and the second the falling off marked by the influence of the American-trained graduates.

(*a*) The Egboes (Ibos) are considered the most imitative and emulative people in the whole of Western Africa; place them where you will, or introduce them to any manners and customs, you will find that they very easily adapt themselves to them. Stout-hearted, or, to use the more common phraseology, big-hearted, they always possess a desire of superiority, and make attempts to attain it, or excel others. To them we may well apply the language of Dryden – 'A noble emulation beats their breasts'.

From *West African Countries and Peoples* by Dr James Africanus B. Horton, London, 1868, quoted by Thomas Hodgkin in *Nigerian Perspectives* (An Historical Anthology) pp. 286–7.

(*b*) I like the disciplinary atmosphere of the force and I took many beltings from one Sergeant Krukru Frafra, who was detailed to put us through in drilling. He preferred to dole out punishment to us, by slapping our cheeks, when the command 'Eyes Right' was given during drill practice. Also I was fond of the classroom work because, in addition to studying the *Police Manual,* we had to learn the fundamentals of criminal law and procedure and the law of evidence. Captain J. R. Barlow, our instructor, took great interest in me, because I was among the leaders of the class. He thought that, other things being equal and after six months' training, I would make the grade and probably be promoted as an Assistant Superintendent.

My Odyssey: An Autobiography by Nnamdi Azikiwe, London, 1970, p. 59.

The most striking thing about the passages is the evidence of a firm structural control exercised by the writer of passage (*a*) over his material, and the absence of this control in passage (*b*). There is a certain deliberateness and unity of exposition in (*a*) which is lacking in (*b*).

The first passage produces the impression of a well-constructed whole with every part dove-tailed into the unified design. It is composed of three sentences, each relevantly related to the others, and each adds something to create the unified effect expected of the well-made paragraph. The first sentence contains two balanced parts, the first a firm, categorical statement; the second part of the sentence explains and elaborates the first. The second sentence is a further elaboration of the statement and illustration, while the third sentence summarizes the statement and its elaboration with a quotation from a respected poet.

There is some complexity in the detailed structure of this passage. For example, the first sentence contains four principal clauses and two subordinate clauses held together by a semi-colon, two commas, one co-ordinating and two subordinating conjunctions. The second sentence displays much flexibility made possible by skilful use of punctuation marks and parentheses. The final sentence is understandably brief; it no longer elaborates or illustrates but merely summarizes.

In the second passage, there is a tumbling out of impressions as they occur to the author, without any detailed or deliberate effort at unified or logical organization. There are four sentences in the paragraph, each different from the others and seeming to stand by itself, independent of the others. The absence of firm structural relatedness is even noticeable in single sentences, giving the impression that one section of a sentence does not quite know what the other section is doing, just as one sentence is hardly aware of its neighbours. For example, in the opening sentence, we are told that the author likes 'the disciplinary atmosphere of the force'. But we cannot easily reconcile this statement with the odd behaviour of Sergeant Krukru Frafra who would slap people's cheeks when they obeyed the order 'Eyes Right'. It must mean that either the people were not obeying the command precisely (in which case this information needs to have been included) or that Krukru Frafra was a plain bully (in which case the phrase 'disciplinary atmosphere of the force' rings pretty hollow and is a clear matter of misinformation). The same kind of inconsistency and lack of relatedness could be established in the remaining sentences.

A more extreme form of this falling-off has been described by a columnist in the *Nigerian Daily Times* of 16 August 1971. The article deals with the linguistic characteristics of Dr Mbadiwe, one of the American-trained graduates of the late 1930s. He observes that 'His (Mbadiwe's) audacious, un-neological coinages stand in evidence as his special contribution to the development of English studies.' The following are among the 'memorable quotables' attributed to Dr Mbadiwe in the study:

> 'Now, continuing the continuity . . .'
> 'Under the Abubakarian government of Nigeria'
> 'Small money does small things, big money does big things'
> 'Today, the field of life insurance means the perpetuation of the family continuity'
> 'When the come comes to become and we all come to close combat, we shall come out.'

It may be argued that Dr Mbadiwe is using language deliberately to shock, to amuse and to draw attention to himself, a typical politician's ploy. But this is the kind of ploy no Black Victorian would have used or accepted. The vulgarity of the thing would have filled him with shame.

It is significant, however, that the Onitsha popular pamphleteers have developed in the shadow of the American-educated graduates and not under the influence of the British-trained coastal aristocrats. Not surprisingly, they have absorbed the linguistic peculiarities of the former rather than of the latter. For them, the 'manhandling' of the English language by the more flamboyant of the American graduates must have presented exciting possibilities which they were to put to the service of the pamphlet literature.

This period from the late 1930s onward, was marked, by intense political activity. It was the era of the soap-box political rhetoricians and spell-binders. Under the excitement of nationalist politics and the anti-colonial struggle there flourished an interest in popular phraseology (one could almost say, phrase-mongering) such as has hardly been equalled since. New literates and readers of popular newspapers picked up new clichés and invented many more. Nationalist politicians inundated the popular ear with an unceasing flow of long-winded and incomprehensible speeches couched in political jargon. The tendency towards thinking and reacting in clichés and slogans developed further during this intensely political age and has persisted ever since. The pages of the pamphlet literature bear eloquent testimony to it. They are sprayed with stock expressions from newspapers, the cinema, romantic magazines, the Bible and other religious works, literature books and so on.

There are however clear indications that the use of big words has never been universally accepted. Side by side with the cultivation of the sonorous style, there is always a trend in the opposite direction, including a tendency to ridicule and deflate the use of high-flown language. Here, for example, are letters which appeared in the *Eagle and Lagos Critic,* IV, 69 (30 June 1888), and which were obviously meant to poke fun at bombast:

Madame – most worthy of admiration! After long consideration and much meditation on the great reputation you possess in the nation, I have a strong inclination to become your relation . . .

On your approbation of this declaration, I shall make preparation to remove my situation to a more convenient station, to profess my admiration, and if such oblation is worthy of observation, and can obtain commiseration, it will be an aggrandisation beyond all calculation of the joy and exultation of

Yours, Sans Dissimulation.

To which the young lady replies:

Sir – I perused your oration with much deliberation at the great infatuation of your imagination to show such veneration on so slight a foundation.

But after examination and much serious contemplation, I suppose your animation was the fruit of recreation or had sprung from ostentation to display your education by an odd enumeration, or rather multiplication of words of the same termination though of great variation in each respective signification.

Now, without disputation, your laborious application in so tedious an occupation deserves commendation: and thinking imitation a sufficient gratification, I am without hesitation,

Yours, Mary Moderation.

The writer is obviously enjoying himself at the expense of the sonorous and bombastic style. Nor was this tendency to satirize bombast restricted to the journals and newspapers. Even while the Black Englishmen dominated in the coastal region and controlled the newspapers and journals, popular anti-theatre groups were growing up to satirize them. In Lagos, for example, the Melo-Dramatic Society staged plays with suggestive titles. One title admonished the audience with unabashed directness, 'Don't Use Big Words'.

In the pamphlet literature also, there has been a clearly marked reaction against bombast. Bombast characters are used by the pamphlet authors as a way of laughing at the predilection for big words.

In Ogali's *Veronica My Daughter,* there is a bombast character, 'Bomber Billy' who, true to his name, bombards everyone within sight with his polysyllabic nonsense words. This is how Bomber describes a bottle of embrocation given to him by the doctor for the treatment of his injured leg: 'I assure you that this is nothing but a cocified agency antipasimodical producing nothing but voscadum, miszcandum and tiscono. This medicine that I have in hand is called the Grand Electrical, Punchutical Demoscandum which cures all diseases incident to humanity.' This could be a parody of medical jargon. Earlier, he describes his fall like this: 'As I was descending from declivity yesterday, with such an excessive velocity, I suddenly lost the centre of my gravity and was precipitated on macadamised thoroughfare.'

The effect is broad comedy. He gives the audience a good laugh, and since no one likes to be a comic butt, many would unconsciously shy away from this kind of language.

There are also instances in which a writer is deliberately using words in a personal or idiosyncratic manner. When this happens, communication between author and reader is impeded. One pamphlet which defies comprehension is Frank E. Odili's *What Is Life* which is 'Dedicated to Moral Regeneration, with a surveyed speculation of living intended for all'. It opens thus: 'It is in fact a point of matter that if life is to be endured perfectly, and in a more enlightening way than burden-like occupancy, it is a rule of general importance that we should apply a solutional thought into its fare, we must at least find it not all too bitter too.' It goes on in this vein for sixty-four pages, defying all clear comprehension by its craggy obscurity. What is so teasing about the author is that he uses everyday words and yet it is difficult to do more than guess at his thought. This is an extreme case, in which preoccupation with the medium and the lack of concern for communication with the reader gives rise to a mere whirl of words. On the whole, the pamphlet authors express their meanings with clarity and remarkable precision. I mention this particular pamphlet because it represents a tendency, a fascination with English words, which in its most advanced manifestation produces a negative result.

Satire of bombast and idiosyncratic use of language, are not confined to the pamphlet authors only. There are a few such representations in the novels and plays of the intellectual West African authors.

Aluko's Catechist-turned-letter-writer, J. Ade Royasin, in *One Man One Wife*, speaks and writes in elaborately balanced diads and triads woven out of words which are sometimes juxtaposed not because they are appropriate but because they sound good in the mouth. Here is the beginning of one of his petitions composed for a client: 'I beg your honour most respectfully and respectively to carefully and patiently peruse these few lines of a tale of woe and persecution and prosecution perpetrated and perpetuated on your Honour's most unworthy servant, to wit, my humble self, Longe of Idoka Village.'

Wole Soyinka's schoolmaster, Lakunle, in *The Lion and the Jewel* is a wordy character. He denounces the payment of bride price as

A savage custom, barbaric, out-dated,
Rejected, denounced, accursed,
Ex-communicated, archaic, degrading,
Humiliating, unspeakable, redundant,
Retrogressive, remarkable, unpalatable . . .

He stops because he has run out of words. He only has 'the Shorter Oxford Dictionary' but when 'the Longer One' (on order) arrives, he will probably compose a longer list!

The fascination which words, written words, have for many West Africans is brought out superbly by Soyinka in *The Road*. Here is how the mad Professor contemplates the meaning and significance of the 'ultimate word' as he gazes on the copy of a crumpled old newspaper:

Somewhere in the granary is the elusive kernel, the Word, the key, the moment of my rehabilitation. There are the cabalistic signs. The trouble is to find the key. Find the key and it leads to the Word. Very strange . . . very strange . . . a rash of these signs arrived lately. Oh God, Oh God, the enormity of unknown burdens, the hidden wisdoms. Say the Word in our time, O Lord, utter the hidden Word. But what do these

mean? These signs were made by human hands. What in the
power of hell do they mean?

If we ignore, for the moment, the vague confusion of the Biblical
'Logos' with the secular quest for the true meaning of the written word
in the Professor's fevered imagination, we see in the passage another
example of the interest which the written word has for new literates in
West Africa, an interest which is excited by the very novelty of
writing and the written word.

This phenomenon is well reflected by Chinua Achebe in that
memorable passage in *No Longer at Ease* in which the hero, Obi
Okonkwo, recalls his father's strong and unwavering belief in the
efficacy and staying power of the written word:

Mr. Okonkwo believed utterly and completely in the white
man. And the symbol of the white man's power was the
written word, or better still, the printed word. Once before
he went to England, Obi heard his father talk with deep
feeling about the mystery of the written word to an illiterate
kinsman:

'Our women made black patterns on their bodies with the
juice of the *uli* tree. It was beautiful, but it soon faded. If it
lasted two market weeks it lasted a long time. But sometimes
our elders spoke about *uli* that never faded, although no one
had ever seen it. We see it today in the writing of the white
man. If you go to the native court and look at the books
which clerks wrote twenty years ago or more, they are still as
they wrote them. They do not say one thing today and
another tomorrow, or one thing this year and another next
year. Okoye in the book today cannot become Okonkwo
tomorrow. In the Bible Pilate said: "What is written is
written." It is *uli* that never fades.'

Examples can be multiplied. In West Africa, writing and the
written word elicit from new literates a wide variety of attitudes
ranging from simple excitement to superstitious awe. The intellectual
authors draw attention to this peculiarity in a semi-facetious, semi-
satirical tone while the popular writers epitomize it.

In spite of their self-confidence in venturing into an area of activity
where only a few of those better prepared by education and experience
have set foot, the popular authors show a surprising modesty in
publicly acknowledging the weaknesses in their use of the English

language and inviting constructive suggestions from readers. This apologetic attitude is not found in the novels and plays of the intellectual authors. These authors, most of whom are university graduates, write English with confidence and competence.

This passage from the Introduction to H. O. Ogu's *How to Fall in Love With Girls* is fairly representative of this tendency of the popular authors to solicit helpful critical comments about their works. It says: 'May I inform my readers and those who are interested in the field of literature that fair and constructive criticism are highly welcomed in this Book.' Even a relatively sophisticated pamphleteer like Ogali A. Ogali makes this appeal to the reader in the Preface to *Veronica My Daughter*:

> May I inform Readers and those who are well advanced in the field of Literature that this is my first attempt in writing a drama. I may have my faults – numerous as such – as any other dramatist has had – even Shakespeare, the World's greatest dramatist – but the idea is there which may represent the writer's intention. Fair and constructive criticisms, I am sure, can make me improve in the art of play writing and be able to present dramas which may receive public applause when staged.

This tendency to invite constructive criticism shows how seriously the pamphlet authors take their writing. They are not content to go on producing bad works if they can help it. As apprentices in the business of creative writing who have had, in most cases, no more than a few years of sustained study of English language and literature, they know that they have far to go to master the language and literary techniques.

It is true that many of the works contain faulty syntax, wayward punctuation and chaotic spelling. But the writers need not be unduly perturbed. That they have been able to write at all has been largely due to their lack of self-conscious fear of breaking the rules. Because they are in a state of relative linguistic innocence, they are able to venture into fields where fastidious users of the language would have found it difficult to set foot. Their works also owe their quality of freshness and sparkle to their authors' audacious handling and mishandling of English idiom.

This is borne out by numerous examples in the pamphlets, especially in those cases in which the authors while meaning one thing succeed in saying something totally different, as in such expressions as

a bird of roses
a ball in a china shop
head over feels in love
east and west name is best. ·
Some of the mistakes are a result of poor editorial work by not-so-very-competent compositors. Genuine mistakes very often result from the authors' inadequate grasp of the idioms and proverbs of the English language.

Thus, a character in Iguh's *Tshombe of Katanga* says. 'Why should we continue to swallow his pronouncements hook and sinker?' Again, when a character in Olisa's *About the Husband and Wife Who Hate Themselves* says to his wife, 'I have nosed the perfume. It is my favourite chop,' we are amused by the transference of the cosmetic smell of perfume to the pleasant smell of cooking. When someone says in Agbugba's *The Wonders of Love*, 'Mother, let us stick the hammer on the nail' we know what English idiom is meant but we also recognize that the speaker has not used it right.

The pamphlet authors sometimes deliberately distort fixed English expressions in order to produce comic or humorous effects. Expressions such as

... let us call a spade a spade and not a fork
... call a spade a spade and nothing but a spade
... the sweetness of the food is in the tasting
... nothing venture, nothing have
... we must not cut our noses to make our faces fine

cannot altogether be attributed to the authors' ignorance of English idiom. They are a transformation of existing idioms, and imply an imaginative transformation. They show not only that the user is aware of standard idioms but that he has enough 'sophistication' to be able to play around with them.

The effect of the pamphlet literature thus owes much to the linguistic innocence of the popular authors and something also to their tendency to take liberties with the language, compelling it to perform in a manner beyond more orthodox users. The result, as Professor Collins has established in his essay is that the pamphlets teem with 'happily misunderstood words and idioms, lucky violations of vocabulary restrictions, vocabulary novelties, fresh figures of speech, unorthodox functional shifts, inkhorn terms, sprung syntax, etc.'

It is necessary to distinguish actual mistakes from deliberate stylistic or idiosyncratic innovation in the pamphlet literature. For example, some authors make their illiterate or semi-literate characters speak in West African 'pidgin' English. Sometimes, they take pains to explain such idiosyncratic usages in their prefaces. Olisa, for example, adds this explanation at the end of his preface to *About the Husband and Wife Who Hate Themselves*: 'Going through this book, you will come across words like "Itankio" meaning "Thanks" and "Awelican" meaning "Welcome". Bear these in mind, don't forget, otherwise you read certain passages without satisfactory understanding.'

In *Veronica My Daughter* we have already noticed the use of a bombast character, Bomber Billy, for a comic effect. In one scene, after one of Bomber's wordy explosions, a character whispers to his neighbour: 'I told you he is fond of big words. Do you understand him?' An aside such as this is directed to the audience as much as to the character concerned, and is calculated to 'inform' the audience about the idiosyncracy of the particular character and to distinguish him from the 'normal' characters. This is a device widely employed by Shakespeare in his plays and therefore not unfamiliar to the pamphlet authors.

We have also deliberate cases of parody of well-known texts. An example is the first line of the poem in Highbred Maxwell's *Public Opinion on Lovers* in which the Shakespearean 'Life's but a walking shadow' is transformed into 'Love is a walking shadow'. More sustained examples are the two parodies of the 23rd Psalm in Ogali's *Mr. Rabbit is Dead,* really delightful pieces which bring out the love of bombast as well as the author's skill in the organization of words. Here is the parody, entitled 'Government'. It carries a sharp satirical sting:

> Government is my shepherd, I am in want.
> He maketh me to lie down in prison yard.
> He leadeth me beside hold of firms.
> He restoreth my doubts in the crown colony system of Government.
> He leadeth me in the paths of helplessness.
> For the sake of his official redtapison,
> Yea, though I work through the shadow of perpetual economic and political servitude,
> I fear all evil for it seems thou art against me.
> Thou preparest a reduction in my salary in the presence of my economics.

Thou anointest my head with income tax.
Thy politicians and profiteers, they frighten me.
My expenses runneth over my income.
Surely oppression and misery shall follow me
All the days of Crown Colony system of administration
And I shall live in poverty and misery in my own God-given
home for ever . . .
Amen.

One important area where the inexperience of some of the pamphlet authors shows most starkly is in their handling of dramatic form. The dramatic form requires close concentration of effect and structural neatness and makes a more strenuous demand on the popular writers than straight-forward narrative. Some of the plays spread and sprawl in formless prolixity, giving more the effect of a village market activity than of an organized and disciplined action. The worst example of a structurally weak play is Okenwa Olisa's *About the Husband and Wife Who Hate Themselves* with its twenty-nine speaking characters and fifteen scenes. In this play, there is a scene dealing with a drug-peddler and a charlatan, and involving a mêlée. It is totally unrelated to the rest of the play and is interposed for no reason that one can see except, perhaps, that it is meant to liven up the action. This is hardly necessary, since a lot of violent exchanges have already taken place in the mainstream of the drama.

But, in spite of the naivety and innocence in the pamphlet authors' use of language and organization of form, many of them are familiar with the conventions of publishing, including the use of prefaces and introductions to clarify intentions. They also seek to protect their works from libel laws by stating explicitly that the characters and situations they deal with are 'purely fictitious'. Their knowledge of publishing conventions is not surprising, since many of them are journalists and publishers; nor is the precaution against libel charges unnecessary, since many of the incidents dealt with in the pamphlets are taken from actual life situations. The danger of libel action may be greater than the reader imagines. Take this statement in Egemonye's *Broken Engagement* for example: 'I wish it to be clearly understood that every character in this novel is imaginary. No real person is ever delineated and only by accident can anybody bear the same name as one of my "players".'

This warning from the author of *The Adventures of the Four Stars* is even more emphatic. 'The characters, places and names mentioned in this book are the author's creative imagination. If by chance they coincide with a place, direct resemblance or allusion with any group of persons, individual or Society dead or alive; in no way must it be taken as a material reality.' And so is Miller O. Albert, in his preface to *Rosemary and the Taxi Driver* when he writes: 'All characters in this novel, are all round imaginary. Note, none is real. It is no true story and therefore concerns nobody in anyway. Whoever hits his head at the ceiling does it at his own personal risk.'

This too emphatic insistence on the imaginariness of the characters suggests that the incident described is based on a real situation and that some of the names in the story may be those of actual people. The cautious statement of the author is therefore meant to disarm would-be litigants.

Given the modest educational background of many of the pamphlet authors, and the fact that the tradition of creative writing was only just beginning to develop in West Africa when the popular authors invaded the field, one is impressed by the quality and range of the work already produced. A proper approach by commentators on the pamphlets would be to put forward sympathetic and constructive criticism and not to seek to undermine the enthusiasm of popular authors by unrestrained fault-finding and carping criticism. A sensitive commentator must regard the pamphlet literature with a feeling of gratitude and justifiable pride. It is a considerable achievement. If Shakespeare, the favourite author of the Onitsha Market pamphleteers, were to read the pamphlets, he would recognize in them one of the major problems which he and his contemporaries had to grapple with: how to borrow foreign influences and traditions and of accommodating them to local material and experience. He would see that the Onitsha Market authors have created a literature which has a certain autonomy and authenticity, in spite of borrowings from the outside.

8   The Newspaper and the Cinema

The newspaper and the cinema are major influences on the Onitsha Market literature. This is no surprise, given that both the newspaper and the cinema have enormous popular appeal. Their popularity depends to a very large extent on their accessibility, and this in turn has had to depend on their mode of operating on their audiences.

Certain facts about the newspaper and the cinema as media of communication should be taken notice of here. After four years of systematic education in any language, a man is able to read a newspaper written in that language. Which is another way of saying that a large section of a country's literate population has available to it that country's newspapers. Furthermore, because of their topicality and because they make relatively little demand on the concentration and mental energy of readers, newspapers have a very wide audience. As for the cinema, its appeal to the visual and auditory faculties, as well as its non-insistence on literary skill, combine to make available to it the largest audiences of all.

In West Africa the cinema commands this largest audience of all the mass media, while the local newspapers are read by thousands of the highly educated as well as new literates. This has a direct bearing on the discussion of the Onitsha pamphlet literature, and the impact of the mass media on its development. Both the newspaper and the cinema are familiar to the authors of the pamphlets, as well as to the people about whom and for whom they write. Both therefore affect the pamphlet literature. We may well begin with the newspaper.

The tendency of newspapers to popularize certain ideas and expressions and to 'demote' them to clichés everywhere has always been recognized; but in Africa this tendency is even more pronounced because the scope of people's reading is so narrow. For a large number of people, newspapers remain the only reading matter. They pore over newspaper pages as if they contained the rarest words of wisdom. That means that new ideas thrown up in the newspapers are soon picked up, committed to memory and sometimes put to new use by avid newspaper readers.

We shall discuss a few examples here. The 'fundamental human rights' were enunciated in the United Nations Charter and later popularized by the nationalist press and politicians in West Africa during the struggle for independence in the 1940s. The idea gained common currency and was taken up by the pamphlet authors. In the popular pamphlets young women resisting their parents' attempt to impose undesirable husbands on them are made to appeal to it. Other similar expressions popularized by the newspapers are 'That man should not be a wolf to man' (this is the motto of a daily newspaper in Onitsha), or phrases like 'Cock and bull stories'. These and many more like them occur in the pamphlets. Even a relatively new cliché like 'the wind of change' has found a place in the popular booklets. It gained currency after the former British Prime Minister Harold Macmillan's historic speech in the South African Parliament in 1960. Thus, in Thomas Iguh's *The Last Days of Lumumba,* a character is reported as saying 'We have been ruled and exploited by Belgium for donkey long years, but now, I am sorry to say that the wind of change will in no time blow across this great nation of ours.' Ogali A. Ogali, one of the most devoted users of popular newspaper clichés, writes of a girl who has deserted her imprisoned husband: 'With Okonkwo in jail, Caro quickly changed her name back to her maiden names, and what a wind of change!' (*Caroline, the One-Guinea Girl*). In the same novelette we have such newspaper-disseminated phrases as 'Operation U.K.' (to indicate a girl's effort to get to the United Kingdom at all costs), and 'white college' (to denote the prison yard).

The influence of the newspaper is most evident in the large number of pamphlets dealing with political events and personalities in (and sometimes outside) Africa. This in itself is not surprising, since the growth of the popular press in Africa was inextricably bound up with the fight by African nationalists against European imperialism. Leaders of this fight became continental heroes and were lionized in the popular press. The pages of the popular newspapers were crammed with stories (some of them true, many of them apocryphal) about the exploits of nationalist politicians. Pamphlet authors, as reflectors of popular attitudes and situations, could not ignore a subject of such interest to their readers. The scope of their works concerned with these subjects is indicated by such titles as *Dr Zik in the Battle for Freedom* (T. O. Iguh); *Zik of Africa, His Political Struggles for Freedom of the Black Race* (Chike Mbadugha); *Boy's Life of Zik, the President of Nigeria Republic* (M. Okenwa); *Heroes of New Africa: Zik, Genius of Today* (Okwu Izuogu); *Dr Nkrumah in the Struggle for Freedom* (T. O. Iguh); *Dr Julius Nyerere: A Profile* (T. I. Nduka); *The Struggles and Trials of Jomo Kenyatta* (T. O. Iguh); *Sylvanus Olympio* (R. I. M. Obioha); *The Life of Alhaji Adegoke Adelabu* (O. A. Ogali).

Obviously, the people written about are those in whom considerable interest has been built up in the local press, and who have captured the imagination of popular writers and their readers. It is the element of wonder which is often appealed to, and these African nationalists are often invested not only with supreme sagacity in their dealings with the mighty imperialists but also with magical and supernatural powers which enable them to survive.

The leader most mythicized in the pamphlet literature is Nnamdi Azikiwe, the first President of Nigeria. This has to do, as Lindfors has pointed out in 'Heroes and Hero-Worship in Nigerian Chapbooks', with his being a local boy who made good, a successful Igbo from Onitsha, the home of the pamphlet literature. But there is more to it than that. Zik's impact was a national one because his was the first attempt to mobilize the evolving modern class of urban clerks, teachers and artisans into a mass political movement, and to infuse into them a spirit of nationalism. His innovating, sensationalizing style in the press, pointed out by Increase Coker in the article already referred to, created his reputation in the eyes of the generality of the people. His spell-binding, rhetorical style of speaking and writing helped to fire popular imagination which, once roused, vested him with all sorts of virtues and powers, possible and impossible.

Okenwa Olisa's pamphlet, *Many Things You Must Know About Ogbuefi Azikiwe and Republican Nigeria* published in 1964, reflects some of the popular belief in the fantastic qualities attributed to Azikiwe. Thus, giving the simple historic estimate of Zik's earlier position in Nigerian politics in the highly inflated language typical of popular admiration, Olisa writes: 'It is a general fact, and an accepted one, as well, that Nnamdi Azikiwe – "Zik" – was Nigeria's No. 1 hero in the political emancipation of the Federal Republic of Nigeria.'

Azikiwe's progress through elementary and grammar school, his attempt to stow away, his scholastic successes in the United States, and early brushes with the British administration on his return to Nigeria are seen with the fascinated eye of hero-worship. Zik is projected as an *enfant terrible* to the colonial administration. He is given magical and supernatural powers. Olisa reports that Zik was regarded as a spirit who could change into a fly or any other creature when he met a fatal danger. He was said to be beyond human destruction. These ideas were greatly reinforced by the numerous tales clustering round the story of an assassination plot against him in 1951. To the generality of the common people, in those days of hectic myth-making, the question was always whether Zik was to be regarded as a mere mortal or as a spirit. To which Olisa volunteers the answer that Zik is indeed 'a pure human being with extensive stock of knowledge, talent, democracy etc.'

One element of the mythicizing of nationalist leaders has been their investment in the pamphlets with messianic qualities. Each of them – Azikiwe, Nkrumah, Lumumba, Kenyatta – is built into a Christ-like figure. Their self-sacrificing heroism is insisted on and woven into the fabric of 'passion' story. For instance, in Ogali's *Patrice Lumumba,* Lumumba is made to address his captors like this:

> You have all sold our hard won freedom back to Belgium and
> Western Powers. I know you have all vowed to treat me
> shamefully as did the Jews to our Saviour . . . You have sold
> the Republic of Congo to Belgium and the Western Powers
> for thirty pieces of silver. But was the Son of Man not sold for
> that amount by his people?

Elsewhere in the same booklet, Lumumba reproaches Tshombe, who has just slapped him, with 'Was Jesus not slapped even by those who dared not tread where he did?'

The parallel between the lives of nationalist politicians in Africa and the life of Christ is an important aspect in the creation of the charisma of those leaders – a process which they themselves immensely assisted. The political rhetoric of the anti-imperialist campaign period was redolent with messianic references, which worked on the high biblical consciousness of the masses to create the popular estimation of nationalist leaders. Here, for example, is a speech taken from a selection of speeches by Azikiwe. It is heavily laden with references to Calvary, Golgotha, and Gethsemane:

> Gethsemane was there to be conquered. Golgotha was there
> to be trodden under the feet of man. Calvary was to be
> overcome. And when a son of the new Africa is faced with the
> travails and tribulations of Gethsemane, and Golgotha and
> Calvary, there is no need for the spirit to weaken. At this
> stage of my life, I cannot be mere flesh. I cannot be part of the
> corruptible phase of man's organism. I am a living spirit of an
> ideal – the ideal of man's humanity to man. I am a living

spirit of an ideology – the ideology of the effacement of man's inhumanity to man.

(Zik: A Selection from the Speeches of Nnamdi Azikiwe. Cited by Adrian Roscoe in *Mother is Gold* (A Study in West African Literature), Cambridge, 1971, p. 158).

The same close parallel between the incidents in the lives of nationalist politicians and the life of Christ was seen in many Gold Coast newspapers on the imprisonment of Nkrumah and his colleagues before the independence of the then Gold Coast. One heated editorial simply announced, 'GBEDEMA GOES TO CALVARY' and then proceeded to chronicle the tribulations of the saviours of the people and ending with a prophecy of impending resurrection to political power.

The popular pamphlet authors had numerous sources from which to draw in building up their nationalist heroes. The newspapers, the radio and other mass media were the main source, but these were amply reinforced by the soap-box, the pulpit, and above all, by the biblical tradition. The political heroes themselves were not slow to play on the popular imagination, especially its preference for the fantastic and the picturesque as against the ordinary and the realistic; they vested themselves with qualities which were thereafter elaborated and mythicized. They sometimes inspired the spread of apocryphal tales about themselves and their accomplishments. In this endeavour the organs of mass information were invaluable and they were exploited to the full to influence the formation of public opinion.

Even though most of the 'political' pamphlets deal with Africans, a few are about illustrious 'topical' non-Africans. There are, for example, booklets on *The Life Story and Death of John Kennedy* and *The Life History and Last Journey of President John Kennedy* (both by W. Onwuka), based on snatches of information about the murdered American President gleaned from the press and radio. Another pamphlet, *The Trial of Hitler* (S. P. Oloyede), reports a fictitious trial of the German dictator and owes much to the reports of the Nuremberg trials and that of Eichmann.

The major post-independence African crises are widely covered in the pamphlets, especially the Congo and the Nigerian crises. On the Congo crisis of 1960, we have such titles as: *The Last Days of Lumumba* (T. O. Iguh); *Patrice Lumumba* (O. A. Ogali); *How*

94   *African Popular Literature*

Lumumba Suffered in Life and Died in Katanga (Okenwa Olisa); *The Life Story and Death of Lumumba* (O. Olisa); *The Trials and Death of Lumumba* (Felix N. Stephen); *How Tshombe and Mobutu Regretted After the Death of Mr. Lumumba* (F. N. Stephen); *Tshombe of Katanga* (T. O. Iguh); *The Ghost of Lumumba* (Ogali A. Ogali). Each of the pamphlets dramatizes some aspect of the crisis. On the Nigerian crises: there are: *N.C.N.C. and N.P.C. in Political War Over 1963 Census Figures* (O. Olisa); *The Iniquity and Trial of Awolowo* (C. H. A. Obi Nwala); *The Bitterness of Politics and Awolowo's Last Appeal* (G. H. A. Obi Nwala); *The Famous Treason Trial of Awolowo and 23 Others* (W. Onwuka); *The Complete Story and Works of Military Government and Nigerian Current Affairs, The Record of Northern and Western Crisis in Nigeria since Army Takeover* (C. O. Uwadiegwu); *The Western Nigeria Crisis and the Army Takeover 1966* (Anon.).

A detailed study of these pamphlets shows that as well as fostering political consciousness the newspapers have contributed considerably to the conditioning of the attitudes of their readers to political events in Africa and elsewhere. To take for example one of the Congo pamphlets, Olisa's *How Lumumba Suffered in Life and Died in Katanga,* there is no doubt that the chief characters bear out the author's biased opinion of them, and it turns out that what the writer thinks of them reflects opinions widely current in the nationalist press about the *dramatis personae* in the Congo tragedy. Tshombe is portrayed as a wicked and almost inhuman adversary who shoots Lumumba as he kneels down in prayer outside a Katanga jail and then repairs to a pub to celebrate his infamous triumph. He earns the opprobrious name, 'Monger,' because his motives are regarded as mercenary. Dag Hammarskjold is described as 'one of the main brains behind Lumumba's death'. Lumumba is the stainless hero: patriotic, brave and full of virtue. Before his death, he delivers a long patriotic speech which ends with these defiant words addressed to the persecutor, Tshombe: 'You can slap, beat, starve and kick me like a football, but I won't ask for mercy.'

What the 'political' pamphlets show is the immense power which the press has acquired to influence public opinion and form the mental and imaginative horizons of people in West Africa, especially those who are not likely to travel beyond their immediate vicinities or to grapple with the higher reaches of political problems. In complete contrast is the handling of the subject of politics by sophisticated

West African authors. In place of the popular authors' hero-worship of nationalist politicians, the intellectual novelists and playwrights like Chinua Achebe (*A Man of the People*), Gabriel Okara (*The Voice*), Wole Soyinka (*Kongi's Harvest*) show politicians as corrupt, using their privileged position to corrupt and oppress the people. There is nothing heroic about politicians as portrayed in serious West African literature.

As one of the major influences moulding the attitudes of contemporary West Africans in things like dress, romantic love and material success, the cinema contributes directly in defining the world of values of the pamphlet literature. Commercial films especially (which must be distinguished from documentary or educational films) are aimed at entertainment rather than fostering the adoption of new attitudes, values and styles of life among those who are in search of the 'modern'. The more these films sensationalize the attitudes, styles and values emanating from the West, the more they appeal to the popular imagination and stimulate imitation.

It is the films which portray the glamour and opulence of Hollywood, the devil-may-care toughness of the heroes, and the slick efficiency of the gang-leaders which are most admired. The man who is successful with women, the successful gangster, the man of action, the man of the world who drinks hard, chain-smokes, overdresses and talks tough is the hero after whom film-going adolescents and those adults who are wholly committed to acquiring the new style of life model their lives. Western commercial films are for such people a school where they imbibe, through suggestion, the material side of Western life which they regard as synonymous with progress and civilization. As well as European and American films, there has been, since the war, a large influx of Indian films with their 'romantic' stories and an element of magic and the supernatural, which appeal very much to the popular imagination.

Because the popular pamphleteers reflect life on the level at which people are most open to such suggestive influences, their writing conveys unmistakeably the direct influence of the cinema. This influence appears in different ways. In the first place, some expressions used by characters in the pamphlets are taken from films. Hence the expression 'Look, old man, play cool' in Ogali's *Eddy the Coal-City Boy* or 'Right, you just get this, and get it straight ...' (Chiazor: *Back to Happiness*) which preludes a girl's quarrel with a despised lover. Some characters emulate the style of tough film-actors, as in this exchange between a forward young lady and her timid lover:

> *Eliza*: Chima. I think you ain't feeling comfortable.
> 'Well', Chima hummed.
> *Eliza*: Say on with certainty. Play your rough. Assume this is an opera. Calling on for your own art. Aren't you a generate male?

West African 'intellectual' authors poke fun at the predilection of some youngsters to imitate the speech and behaviour of movie gangsters. In Wole Soyinka's *The Road,* for example, there is a small-time gang-leader called 'Say Tokyo Kid' who is depicted as an African who has become a miniature American 'tough'. This is how Soyinka introduces this character in the play:

> (Enter Say Tokyo Kid)
> *Say T*: (Looks round a little worriedly):
> I ain't late am I?
> *Salubi*: Say Tokyo! Say Tokyo Kid!
> *Say T*: Salubi salubrity! Say man, everybody garrered round the goorold place. How's business kid?
> *Salubi*: Say Tokyo Charranooga Shoe-shine Boy!
> *Say T*: Thas me. I'm allright boy. (Sees the officer and recoils.
> Makes to pull an imaginary gun from his belt).

Soyinka's excellent eye for the absurd in contemporary Nigeria has not missed the effect of lurid American gangster films on some people. Cyprian Ekwensi, also explores some aspects of this impact in his urban novels. Denis of the underworld in *Jagua Nana* is a pocket edition of the big American gang-leader; his style of living, if less opulent, still reflects the excitement and carelessness of those who cynically regard society as a gold mine. The effect of the cinema can also be seen in Ekwensi's *Burning Grass,* which reads in places like an embryonic Western, with Fulani adversaries fighting it out with swords and daggers instead of shooting at one another with guns.

The popular authors are not far behind in portraying gansters who pattern their lives and actions on film gangsters. For instance, Miller O. Albert in *Rosemary and the Taxi Driver* describes the effect of the cinema on one of his characters: 'Okoro was a film goer. He knew himself that to change a car was an English method of bringing confusion into crime'. Alex. Obiorah Okeke explicitly says in the introduction to his play, *I'll Rather Break My Sword and Die*: 'I

developed the sense of dramas by daily attendance of film shows and
by reading novels, booklets and daily newspapers.'

J. A. Okeke Anyichie's *Adventures of the Four Stars* is closely and
consciously patterned on the lives of cowboys and movie-gangsters.
The book has a picture of a cowboy on the cover, and the author
leaves one in no doubt that he is out to create characters and
situations based on those he has seen at cowboy and gangster films.
His introduction speaks for itself:

> It is with profound practical experience of what happened in
> the Old Western Countries, the era of Texas gunslingers, the
> Cow Boys and the Red Indians; the idea with which I set to
> write the *Adventures of the Four Stars* depicting African guys
> in a set of Old Lagos Suburb.
>
> In the Western Countries of America they call it Wild Old
> West, but here in Africa, it is the era of the dope addicts and
> peddlars; the Bad Boys of Tinubu Square, the Wild Takwa
> Bar-Beach Boys and the jayi-jayi addicts of Ido-Oro suburb.
> Read of them in thrilling and fascinating adventures packed
> in one.

Elsewhere in the same pamphlet, the narrator considers that his
Nigerian imitation cowboys and gansters fall short of the originals:

> I let my mind draft to different types of false imaginations. I
> was just wondering what it means to be tough. The thought of
> some old celebrated Western Films I used to go (to) began to
> dawn upon me. I thought of Four Guns to Mesa; Tony
> Curtis in adventures of Robin Hood; the Carribean Gold
> and all sorts of Western Cow Boys of yester years.
>
> But here is black Africa. Where the idea of old Wild
> West of America, the days of gun slingers and hired gun
> men, was a mere dream. With these thoughts I decided that it
> would take another decade to produce tough guns. I mean
> like Robert Wanger, Billy the Kid, Jessy James and Durango
> Kid.

The 'tough' talking and 'tough' action which is so widespread in the
popular pamphlets can be traced directly to gangster films. Many
South African short stories published in *Drum* magazine show,
terrifyingly, how deeply the tendency to imitate American gangsters
has permeated the lives of young Africans in the urban ghettoes and
shanty towns of South Africa, stimulating violence, drug-addiction,
and crime. In West Africa, the phenomenon is new, but is spreading

in the urban areas with the ever-increasing influence of the cinema (and of course, industrialization). The Onitsha pamphlet literature bears testimony to that fact.

The association of the cinema with romantic love is equally strong and is equally reflected in the popular pamphlets. This charming passage occurs in R. Okonkwo's *Why Boys Never Trust Money Monger Girls*:

> The film show started at the same time.
> It was a very good and interesting film.
> Joe and Cordelia enjoyed it very much.
> The film was a romancing one and for that it suited their state for love.
> When the actors and actresses in the film kissed themselves, Joe and Cordelia kissed each on their own part.

Again, in C. C. Obiaga's *Boys and Girls of Nowadays,* a character hovering at the brink of bankruptcy is reluctantly dragged to a film show by his girl friend. The affair proves a fiasco but it is worth quoting because it bears out the point being made here. This is how the writer describes it:

> Usually while the film was on and there was a part where there was kissing, Jerry would kiss Obiageli as well. But today Jerry was so absent-minded that he forgot to kiss Obiageli during a kissing part of the film. Obiageli turned sharply to Jerry and asked him why he didn't kiss her. Jerry was unable to answer. 'Jerry, I think you don't love me any longer,' said Obiageli.

Sometimes attendance at film shows destroys the security which young lovers hope to realize by having their romantic aspirations ratified by the film world and its rituals. Such is the case of Jerry and Obiageli. Nwosu's *Miss Cordelia in the Romance of Destiny* gives an even more typical case of the hazards to which relationships are sometimes put when two people in love draw different and contradictory morals from a romantic film. In this case, the lovers have been seeing the film, 'Samson and Delilah'. The effect on the young man is disturbing and he says ruminatively to his girl friend, 'Did you see another proof to the fact that women have been and will always remain man's greatest source of failure?' The young lady greets this observation with a frown, for she recognizes in it rebuke of herself for dragging him away from his homework. Some of the love situations are diversified by such streaks of irony. Not even the cinema, with its glamourization of romantic love, can totally exorcize the pains which sometimes attend personal relations.

One result of the influence of the cinema is a change in the criterion of beauty. Film actors and actresses are now the models of beauty for boys and girls. The older generation of African men preferred their women big-framed, tall, with erect carriage, but 'modern' young men prefer their women slim, petite and excitingly made up.

Women used to have to work on the land and carry heavy burdens. This may have helped to determine the criterion in African agricultural societies. Such traditional practices as the grooming of young nubile women in fattening chambers may well reflect an aestheticization of an event which had its roots firmly entrenched in economics. The current ideal of beauty differs so conspicuously, especially in relation to size, that what pleases the traditionally-oriented eye may actually be repellent to the 'modern', cinema-conditioned eye.

The popular writers' ideal of feminine beauty is the film actress, and when they describe beautiful women, the wasp-waisted, mascara-groomed, scarlet-lipped woman is their model. But because many of the writers are incapable of finding the appropriate words to describe her, they resort to expedients which are often ludicrous. This is sometimes also the case with their attempts to describe handsome males as this brief extract from Justin Ezimora's *The Lady That Forced Me to be Romantic* shows:

> She said that I was wonderfully handsome, my eyes blue, my hair golden and to crown all that, I was so far the best mannered lad she ever met.
>
> In reply I told her that her teeth were as white as snow, her hair like those of a mermaid, her nose pointed, her neck stretched out and attractive and lastly, her general appearance like that of Eve, the first queen on earth. She gave me a warm handshake and vanished.

The features described here are obviously more appropriate to Europeans than to Africans. This is a constant discrepancy in the pamphlet literature.

The popular authors excel in describing the effect of beauty on its beholder. They are then most sure, because most vague. A good example is the opening passage of Ogali A. Ogali's *Caroline the One Guinea Girl*:

> Caroline was an interesting object. She was adored by men – young and old, rich and poor.

In plain language, Caroline was a paragon of beauty. Her
smiles sent many young men to the money-lenders.

What for?

Well, the bills – in guineas – must be paid . . . Caro's
acrobatic waist seemed to contain a box of magnetism.

Result?

Men who saw her 'throw steps' as she moved along the
road generally remarked 'Oh dear! Oh dear! What a nice and
attractive waist, I must make a chase!'

'What a pontiac' men said whenever they were chanced to
have a camera look at Caro's nicely set breasts through her
nylon blouse.

Her nose?

The Creator was rather very kind and careful when it was
made.

Neck?

Good Heavens! Caro's neck was almost six inches long
and how crazy were men when they watched her as she turned
her neck in order to respond to a caller's greetings.

'Your eyes are rather very romantic, dear Caro,' men
remarked times without number. She was at her most
romantic form when she 'cut her eyes' in order to entice
men.

Caroline is a temptress and a good-time girl who lives by exerting
her physical attraction over men. This attraction might evaporate if it
were described in concrete terms. The general allusiveness of the
description as 'a paragon of beauty', 'a box of magnetism', and 'a
pontiac' whose appearance would drive men 'to the money-lenders',
leaves the work of perfecting the image to the imagination of the
reader. And since the imagination in such matters can be relied upon
to prefer the poetic to the objective, allusion proves the best device for
describing a provocative, seductive kind of beauty. This is the
technique, we all recognize, of the 'romantic' magazine which specializes in the cult of seduction.

Some pamphlet authors go beyond allusive treatment of the
physical appearance of their characters. They sometimes dwell on
their attention to their toilet, as in Ogu's *How a Passenger Collector
Posed and Got a Lady Teacher in Love*. Here is an example:

Diana coiled her hair in twines and appeared like a stately
tower. Her lips were painted red with lip-stick, while her two

breasts appeared like two budded roses. Her nose stood
straight like that of an Indian film star and lastly but not the
least, the face was fancied with the best make-ups that you
could not dream of.

The effect is relatively crude. There are Biblical clichés such as 'a
stately tower' and 'budded roses'; while the face 'fancied with the best
make-ups' might look like a masquerader's; but, this is some attempt
at a more concrete description.

The intellectual authors, unlike the popular ones, have only scorn
for the uncritical acceptance of the 'modern', cinema-oriented idea of
beauty and 'fashion'. To Achebe, for example, the 'made-up' girls of
nowadays are 'painted dolls'. Soyinka laughs at the whole business
through his misguidedly 'modern' hero, Lakunle, in *The Lion and the
Jewel*. Lakunle's idea of 'fashion' is represented by

High-heeled shoes for the lady, red paint
On her lips. And her hair is stretched
Like a magazine photo.

Many of the pamphlets carry photographs of European and Indian
filmstars on their cover pages. This device is borrowed from the
Indian popular pamphlets on which the African equivalents were
originally modelled. The practice has been extended by the inclusion
of photographs and drawings of young African men and women.
Photographs of famous filmstars are easily available in their hundreds
in market stalls and local photographers' display boxes and so are
available to the pamphlet authors. Some of them are used as
decoration for the backs of hand mirrors and some are even found in
such unlikely places as tea-packet and other labels.

Reinforcing the influence of the cinema on the Onitsha Market
literature is the part which 'love' songs play in stimulating the idea of
romantic love and supplying many of its clichés. The writers of the
popular pamphlets show awareness of the existence of the record song
books and take many of their sentiments, and sometimes exact
expressions, from the songs. In Ugochukwu Ajokuh's *The Chains of
Love*, for example, most of the school boys and girls are shown to
possess record song books. They place them conspicuously on their
parlour tables and spend a considerable part of their holidays singing
the songs. The title of the booklet itself is taken from a song of the
same name made famous by the American crooner Pat Boone. In
Anya's *She Died in the Bloom of Youth*, a ghost is reported as saying:
'Brush away those tears from your eyes, and try to realize that the

ache in my heart is for you', words taken from 'My Happiness', a popular song in the song book.

Modern 'progress' transforms tradition-bound attitudes and outlooks into those which 'liberate' individuals and invest them with a certain ubiquitous vitality and assertive autonomy. In the long run the history of that progress is the history of the progress of the mass organs of communication – the newspaper, radio, cinema and television – in the broadening of the vistas of human experience. The restless enthusiasm of the pamphlet authors and of the characters they portray in their pursuit of new experience bears witness to the effect of the organs of communication in shaking the stability of the traditional psyche and giving it greater mobility. This enthusiasm is expressed through romantic love, the quest for money and economic opportunities, an interest in politics and a desire for pan-African political solidarity.

There are obviously two sides to the account of this progress towards modernity. On balance, most observers will agree with the pamphlet authors that change is desirable, even though the process may involve pitfalls. We may be tempted to laugh at the pamphlet authors and their crude vision of modern progress fostered by the mass media, but we must remember that, debauched as this vision is, it has the strong advantage of being irresistible. The future belongs to the masses. Those who debase mass tastes and depress the spirit through commercially-inspired media will lose their hold when the people realize that a certain moral austerity is essential for real progress and that the organs of mass communication and education which are the principal instruments of true liberation must be put to proper use by those who share their vision of life and aspiration to modern progress. It is only then that they will become the beneficiaries rather than the victims of these media.

9 Religion and Morals

There is always a moral impulse in the pamphlet literature, a drive implicit or explicit to improve the reader, to teach him a moral lesson or to establish a moral thesis for the edification of society. This impulse the pamphlet literature owed to a combination of two major factors – the traditional and the Christian forms of morality. There is a paradox here. We have consistently deduced from various facets of the pamphlet literature that the popular authors and the audience they write for and about reject traditional values (which they regard as constrictive of individual self expression) and espouse new emergent values which derive largely from Western – Christian concepts and ideas. When we examine the handling of moral issues in the pamphlets, we notice that the kind of moral graph which their actions follow is often defined, at least in part, by the traditional concept of morality. If one adds to this the expression of Christian orthodoxy in explicit practices, then one has a fairly complete picture of the treatment of morality in the literature. The pamphlet authors have not managed to escape the consequences of the two powerful formative influences in the lives of most Africans – oral tradition and Christian missionary education. Let us take the first aspect first.

The combination of entertainment and didactic intent in the pamphlets derives its inspiration from oral tradition. The specific oral tradition most closely imitated is the folktale. Anyone familiar with the folktale tradition in West Africa will be impressed by the close patterning of the pamphlet tales on the folktale form. We all know the procedure at a folktale session. The folktale narrator announces that he has a story to tell. The audience asks him to tell it. Then he tells his story and in the end he draws his moral. In some cases, the moral is so obvious that he does not insult the intelligence of the audience by mentioning it.

The folktale is designed to instruct as well as entertain; hence the need to draw or imply the moral at the end. Furthermore, it is an essential way of introducing young people to the customs of their people, their beliefs and prohibitions, their positive values, their ideas and ideals and everything that constitutes their moral and ethical view of the world. In the popular pamphlets, the authors also announce their narrative or dramatic intentions in prefaces and then proceed with their narratives or dramas. (A number of these prefatory statements have been mentioned in the chapter 'Passport to Happy Life'.) When they get to the end, they draw out their intended morals or omit them where the morals have already been enunciated in the prefaces. In some cases, writers conclude with a moral even after they have already foreshadowed them in the prefaces. Thus, in *Miss Rosy in the Romance of True Love,* the writer concludes his tale by asking the reader what he thinks will save him in the present-day world (which the author obviously sees as a jungle of wickedness). He supplies the answer by admonishing the reader to 'stay contented and don't develop interest in Love, Pleasure and High Society'. The direct appeal to the audience is itself a device well known in traditional oral story telling.

The analogy can be developed in another direction. The moral attitude of many of the written stories seems to be patterned on the moral attitude in folktales. There is often poetic justice which insists that the good should be rewarded and the wicked punished. But the punishment itself is only a transition to the rehabilitation of the offender. In folktale morality the offender is hardly ever left in a state of permanent disgrace and deprivation. He has to suffer, even suffer severely, but then he is rescued and restored, much chastened and refined by his punishment*

Melville Herskovits in his *Dahomean Narratives* is puzzled by what he refers to as the absence of tragic themes in West African folktales. This can be explained by the absence in these tales of anything approaching a Christian hell in which errant souls are damned for all time. In folktales, characters are seldom placed beyond the pale of mercy and salvation.

Many tales in the popular pamphlets reflect the moral outlook of the folktale. We shall illustrate this with Ogali's *Caroline the One Guinea Girl.* In this story the heroine, a brutal prostitute, misuses her beauty and physical accomplishments to exploit men ruthlessly. She is called the 'guinea' girl because that is what she charges. In the midst

---

*I am indebted to Dr Donatus Nwoga for drawing attention to this peculiarity in the pamphlet literature. The actual phrase he uses is 'the graph of African morality.' (See his article in *Transition*.)

of her career, after she has ruined many of her clients, she is suddenly struck down. She becomes pregnant and in procuring an abortion, nearly loses her life. While she is at the abortionist's, her flat is burgled, and she loses all her ill-gotten possessions. She becomes the most wretched of the wretched – her beauty gone, her wealth gone, her young men gone and herself an object of scorn and contempt. That, in modern realistic writing, would have been the end of the story, the moral deeply etched as 'the end of a brutal fille'. She would be made to end her miserable life through some horrible disease or suicide.

But Ogali's story does not end there. Caroline begins a process of rehabilitation. She goes home to her parents in the village. She becomes humble and chaste, and preaches constantly at the local church, drawing elaborate moral lessons from her previous life to warn young girls against the pitfalls of life. Later, one of her rejected suitors returns from Oxford University, and marries her. She becomes a very good wife to him and a model mother to his children.

If we compare Caroline's story with true folktale narratives, especially the story of the obdurate daughter who marries a demon lover and is rescued after going through harrowing experiences, it is clear that the same kind of 'graph of morality' operates. The tale of Niku in Aluko's *One Man One Wife* and that of the Drinkard's wife in Amos Tutuola's *The Palm Wine Drinkard* reinforce the point. In both tales, the girls refuse to marry suitors chosen for them by their parents, an impertinent breach of traditional family custom. The girls choose for themselves husbands who turn out not to be human beings at all. The Drinkard's wife chooses an ordinary skull which had borrowed human parts and clothes from various clients in order to pose as a Complete Gentleman. In Aluko's story, the suitor is a boa constrictor which has changed into human form in order to entice an unfortunate girl. Both girls undergo a nightmare experience but are in the end rescued, one by the Drinkard and the other by a hunter whom she had earlier rebuffed. The moral is clear, disaster overtakes the girl who flouts parental authority in the matter of choosing a husband.

But this begs the question, why do the stories not end with the retribution, why should there be a happy ending? The same kind of answer suggests itself both for the folktales and the pamphlet litera-ture. Both forms, as we saw earlier, are concerned with entertainment as well as in instructing the audience. Now, a happy ending is more consonant with entertainment than a sad ending. The moral lesson of these tales is conveyed in the initial suffering of the errant characters; nothing is gained by protracting pain after it has served its purpose. Thus, just as the Drinkard's wife and Niku are rescued from the hopelessness into which they have plunged themselves, so Caroline, the One Guinea Girl, is rescued from the depth of moral depravity and despair into which she has fallen. The husband who rescues her and gives her a new lease of hope is characteristically called Mr Simplicity, a name straight out of folklore or allegory.

The general tendency described here admits significant exceptions. There are stories in which there is no happy ending, no forgiveness and no reconciliation. The characters who have gone wrong do not succeed in redeeming themselves and swift retribution overtakes and destroys them. Such is the story of the heroine in Speedy Eric's *Mabel the Sweet Honey That Poured Away*. Mabel wanted fast living. She paid the bitter price and embraced painful death at the age of seventeen. By and large, however, 'the graph of African morality' ends in most of these tales on a rising note of optimism, forgiveness, reconciliation and rehabilitation.

There is evidence that the pamphlet authors are aware of the oral tradition and are following it. Oral story-telling is still a living tradition in the villages and in the towns. The schools keep the tradition alive by encouraging story-telling sessions, especially in the lower classes, as part of their curricular activity. Children hold story-telling sessions in their homes and also listen to stories and proverbs told by adults. Some of the pamphlet authors have themselves collected and compiled folktales, proverbs and traditional maxims. In fact, Cyprian Ekwensi, the most urbanized of the novelists and a pioneer of the pamphleteering literature, began with a collection of Igbo folktales. Many later pamphlet authors have followed his example.

From internal evidence, it is clear that the authors use or occasionally refer explicitly to oral tradition in their work. In *Chains of Love*, for example, a character tells his friend, 'If I would start my story like our great grandfathers I would first tell you ... how the tortoise thought he was the wisest man only to remember at last that there is one who knew one thing that he did not know himself', to which his friend replies with impatience, 'I know the story, don't tell it'. Some of the episodes in the novelettes are characteristic of certain well-known folktale episodes and some of the pamphlet characters are typical of folktale heroes. In most West African societies, the trickster is a familiar character. We encounter characters modelled on him in a number of the pamphlets. For example, the servant Jumbo who in *How to Fall in Love with Girls* plays 'hide-and-seek' with his master, robbing him of a whole chicken and making a fool of him, is a character straight from the trickster tales. The same thing is true of Emeka, the lorry park tout, who uses disguise to get even with a girl who had earlier mocked his tattered, work-a-day appearance, in H. O. Ogu's *How a Passenger Collector Posed and Got a Lady Teacher in Love.*

Some of the characters in the pamphlets also reflect oral tradition by quoting traditional proverbs. Rendered into English the result is not always happy. In Iguh's *The Disappointed Lover,* for example, a mother asks her daughter to confess to an illicit love relationship by saying: 'If you begin for day time dey find black goat, when night reach you no go seam.' This is a pidgin rendering of the Igbo proverb which says: 'It is better to look for a dark goat while it is still daylight, because you can't see it when darkness comes.'

It is worth noting that use of oral tradition by the pamphlet authors is not as highly developed as it is in the works of the serious authors of novels, dramas and poetry. The popular authors betray the influence in spite of themselves, while for the intellectual West African authors it is a natural way of expressing the living reality of African life. Finally, the popular authors find they have to support their use of oral tradition with the authority of Christian orthodoxy, while many of the intellectual authors separate oral traditional from Christian matter and sometimes treat them as antithetical, showing Christianity as an active force subversive of the native tradition.

It is no surprise that we find in the popular pamphlet literature a reflection of the triumph of Christian missionary education. The popular authors are committed to, and often ardent propagandists of Christianity. They are, in the main, professing Christians and most, if not all of them, have at some time or other in their education been taught by Christian missionaries. Many of them are or have been mission teachers, in which role they have actively fostered the progress of Christianity and also built up an impressive knowledge of the Bible and the Christian liturgy, which they put to account in their writing. This is particularly true of the better-known authors like Ogali A. Ogali and Okenwa Olisa. It is no wonder that Christian attitudes and principles provide one of the major inspirations of the pamphlet literature, and the Bible one of the chief literary influences.

Christian teaching in West Africa, as elsewhere, has tended to stimulate individualism. In as much as its effect has been to weaken the individual's attachment to the traditional religion which embodied the essence of collective tradition in old Africa, Christianity stimulated the individual to assert his separateness from others, and to pursue his own needs and aspirations. Also, Christian education has tended to infuse in Africans exposed to it a deep sense of unease about traditional African religion, because it is depicted as primitive and obscene. Again, because the popular authors and the new literates for whom they write stand for individual assertion and the promotion of institutions which foster individuality, they see Christianity as a great ally and suspect traditional religion and what it stands for as inimical to the expression of their individuality. So they instinctively feel admiration for the former and hostility to the latter. Furthermore, the mere fact that Christianity is associated with modernity and civilization commends it to these writers, just as the supposed primitiveness of traditional religion discredits it. One distinctive feature of the pamphlets is the pro-Christian sentiment which they foster, and the uncompromising antipathy they manifest towards the principles of the traditional religion.

All this is best shown in the popular authors' treatment of marriage. In their attitude to marriage they tend to show polygamy and customary marriage as monstrous anachronisms and to hold up Christian monogamy and its values as the ideal. Thus, for example in Nwosu's *Miss Cordelia in the Romance of Destiny,* old priestesses who intervene to break up a marriage because of unforeseen traditional impediments are thoroughly abused by the younger characters. They are referred to variously as 'hags' and 'wenches' and their chief spokesman is called a 'she dragon'. The author's sympathy appears to be with the young lovers and against the 'meddlesome' priestesses. In Egemonye's *Broken Engagement* a young man who is about to lose his fiancée to a wealthy suitor reminds her with the Christian marriage concept in mind that 'marriage is a sacrament rather than a civil contract and therefore that she must marry not for money but for love'.

The assent of the popular writers to the Christian idea of marriage is suggested by the fact that all the weddings in the pamphlets are celebrated in church. There are good reasons why this is often so. A church wedding is prestigious, as many sociologists of African social change have established. Secondly, a church wedding, like a court trial, is highly dramatic. The minister's questions and the couple's cryptic answers go down well with an audience because of their dramatic possibilities. These, together with the other reasons mentioned earlier, explain the popularity of church wedding ceremonies in the pamphlet literature.

Here is a typical marriage ceremony described in Ogali's *Veronica My Daughter:*

> Stage Direction: (The procession ends in the Cathedral. The couple and many others take their seats):
>
> *Father Clement:* Mr and Mrs Mike, May God bless you.
>
> *Crowd:* A – men.
>
> *Father Clement:* The daughter of God, do you agree to marry this man?
>
> *Veronica:* Yes, Father.
>
> *Father Clement:* For better or for worse?
>
> *Veronica:* Yes, Father.
>
> *Father Clement:* Can you stand him in all his difficulties?
>
> *Veronica:* Yes, Father.
>
> *Father Clement:* In poverty?
>
> *Veronica:* Yes, Father.
>
> *Father Clement:* In sickness?
>
> *Veronica:* Yes, Father.
>
> *Father Clement:* In joy or sorrow?
>
> *Veronica:* Yes, Father.
>
> *Father Clement:* May God grant His love on you.
>
> *Crowd:* A – men.
>
> *Father Clement:* Seal your promise with a holy kiss (He gives Mr and Mrs Mike a Holy Bible and they kiss it). Leave a living testimony with the Church, my children. (He gives them a register and they sign their names). God be with you.
>
> *Crowd:* A – men.
>
> (Father Clement leaves the altar and others follow: music outside. A group photograph is taken. The procession starts again and ends in Michael's house. The inevitable feasting begins, accompanied at intervals with speeches and drinking of toasts and dancing).

In this ceremony the bridegroom is left completely out of the picture, and there are a few of the author's own variations on an actual marriage ceremony but as a fictionalized rendering which exploits the dramatic effect of the situation and brings out the author's commitment to the Christian ethic, it is well done.

Commitment to Christianity is also expressed in other ways. In Ogali's *Caroline, the One Guinea Girl,* the heroine, abandons her life of prostitution and seeks rehabilitation through religion. She becomes a lay preacher in the best non-conformist tradition, treating her audience to thunderous denunciation of those worldly ephemera which had made her past life so colourful and so full of pain. She admonishes her young listeners thus: 'Listen to what your elders tell you in order to build up a high moral standard. Forget not your Bible and throw not aside your hymn books. Fail not to attend classes and services wherever you may be.'

She launches virulent attacks on men, calling them 'sugar-coated tongues' and similar courtesies. Some of this bad-tempered harangue is of course the neurotic outburst of a self-rejecting former rake, for Caroline, far from being an innocent victim of men's deceit, was a self-corrupted, wilful and capricious young woman who did her best to ruin many of her male admirers. The important thing about her reformation, however, is that it should take place through the Christian religion.

Ogali is not alone among the pamphlet writers in implying that only Christianity can rescue the individual from the despair and hazards of life. Another writer, Justin Ezimorah (whose attitude to Christianity is certainly superstitious) tells the story in *The Lady That Forced Me to be Romantic* of how his hero and five companions being menaced in the dark by three long moving creatures, his hero has the presence of mind to make the sign of the cross and this act expels the fearful creatures. The author's 'Great Lesson' from this incident, and one which he seriously recommends to the reader is: 'Make the sign of the cross any time, especially at the time of danger.' The triumph of Christian education can hardly be more complete.

The triumph of Christianity over the bad life is the theme of Olisa's popular novelette, *Vagabond versus Princess*. In his introduction, entitled 'My Firm Belief' Olisa outlines his intentions as follows: 'I firmly believe that there is All-Mighty Father – the God, and no pain in agony will make me to change my mind. My intention of writing and publishing this booklet is merely to expose and kill spiritually the doubts in the hearts of certain human beings about the existence of God.'

The element of propaganda is strong in the work. Vagabond, the hero, is a hater of Christianity and its values. He lives a life of crime and deceit, and presides over a heretical sect with the Bunyanlike designation of 'Devil's Army'. To him the Christian churches are just 'making hell threats against the sinners simply to gain members of the frightened'. In the end, the forces of law close in on Vagabond and he is brought to trial for his anti-social and anti-Christian activities. 'Angel of God', a key prosecution witness, indicts him for plundering society as well as for his wicked heresy. The court sentences him to carry a stone weighing one ton for seventy-two weeks. Vagabond becomes repentant after a day's punishment and recants his heresy. He is reprieved from the remaining part of his sentence and, as an earnest of his changed life, he is rebaptised Emmanuel Innocent. Henceforth, he goes about proclaiming that 'no sin consciously done will be forgiven', which is meant to warn all those so wrong-headed as to imitate his anti-Christian past. Like Caroline, the One Guinea Girl, Vagabond finds security and a new hope in the accommodating bosom of Mother Church.

The influence of Christian education on the pamphlet literature is also evident in the large number of Biblical quotations and allusions in them. The popular writers quote from the Bible and Christian literature in order to display their knowledge of these things, just as they quote from Shakespeare and the classics to display their knowledge of English literature. Thus, for example, in Chidia's *Her Evening Tales,* two intimate friends are compared to 'David and Jonathan of the Bible', a man is called a 'doubting Thomas' because he refuses to believe the claims of a magician in Ogali's *Okeke the Magician,* while an unfaithful wife making up to her husband's friend is likened to 'the forbidden apple in the Garden of Eden', in Okonkwo's *Never Trust All That Love You.*

The Christian impulse in many of the popular pamphlets is clearly shown in Christian imagery and vocabulary. Temptation, sin, confession, contrition, forgiveness, repentance, and such Christian concepts occur frequently in the writing. For example, in Obioha's *Beauty Is a Trouble,* a woman who has left her husband and only son for the glamour of city life returns to them after several years, 'confesses' her 'sins' of 'infidelity' and receives her husband's forgiveness'.

The mere fact that the popular authors quote from Christian literature with such enthusiasm is an indication of their commitment to Christianity. It is more than a pedantic display of knowledge. The Bible is a living work, and they quote from it not in order to show off their knowledge but in order to ratify their attitudes and actions. It is living to them in a way that Shakespeare and other writers are not, because of the devotional awe they attach to its content. An analogy from secular literature might strengthen an individual view-point by putting beside it a similar view-point expressed by some admired writer in the past, but an analogy from the Bible is sufficient and ultimate justification of the view-point itself.

This passage from *The Lady That Forced Me to be Romantic* shows how strong the influence of the Bible can be on the popular authors. It reads:

> As the Serpent tempted Eve in the Beautiful Garden of Eden, she sat boldly on my arms and begged that she might stay. But at that time I was thinking what to do, and it took me hours – literally hours – to reach any decision. After some time I asked her 'Do you know where you are?' She was gaping at me and was motionless. A bit of mercy creeped into my mind. That does not mean that I have lost my aim. It was that I did not want to use force on her as I decided before. I therefore treated her in a way a modern youth ought to act. I started to ask her many questions.

This is a seduction scene which goes wrong because of the young man's religious scruples. The lady in the story is trying to make up to him but, armed with the authority of the Bible, he is proof against her romantic design. By comparing her to the scriptural serpent and himself to Eve, the potential victim of her wiles, he makes up his mind not to be 'trapped'. He even contemplates throwing her out but decides, on second thought, that is too crude a method for 'a modern youth' to adopt. He therefore matches her 'satanic' cunning with his 'saintly' trifling. In the end nothing comes of the matter. Christianity and the Bible get the better of the forces of darkness.

By way of postscript to this discussion, it is worth remarking that the recent civil war in Nigeria exposed the agents of the Christian religion to severe criticism. During the war, the work of bringing in relief material and distributing it to the war-ravaged people of Eastern Nigeria was undertaken by the Christian missions and their staff. And as might be expected, the quantity of relief that came in was grossly inadequate to the large body of needy people. There were accusations

of inequitable distribution of the supplies, and the clergy of the
different Christian sects who had the responsibility for 'relief' distribution came in for severe criticism. One of the major pamphlet
authors, Ogali A. Ogali, wrote a work titled *No Heaven for the Priest*
which articulates many of the criticisms against the 'relief' priests.
Part of it reads as follows:

> I do not believe that christianity depends on reading the Bible
> from Genesis to Revelation! I do not believe also that it
> depends on attending church services every hour of the day,
> every day of the month and every month of the year.
>
> I believe, and very emphatically too, that christianity
> depends on individual soul.
>
> The Nigerian civil war – 1967 to January 1970 taught us
> that all those who say 'my father, my father, shall never see
> the kingdom of God.'
>
> Throughout the duration of the crisis, events showed that
> most of those in the HOLY ORDERS were the most selfish of
> all the people who belonged to the ring of 'Let's get rich quick'
> and 'Let's help our own relations first!'
>
> Many of them sold the relief materials intended for the
> poor and the needy. Relief materials went to Doctors,
> Lawyers, Engineers, fellow clergymen, very important
> personalities, beautiful girl friends and car owners, in fact to
> all those who had enough and (were) capable of helping
> others. The war-time ignoble activities of these unholy, sorry,
> I mean holy people, simply reminded the poor and the needy
> that the so-called kingdom of God, with all its heavenly
> enchantments, would only be for the rich, the high-ups and
> their girl friends.
>
> This is true, very true indeed!
>
> When I remember how the poor and the needy suffered
> during the crisis because they could not get a penny relief;
> when I remember how certain people became *relief*
> themselves, able to feed their dogs and cats with tinned
> food and milk in preference to the suffering masses; and
> when I remember how these holy men, the servants of God,
> cheated the public, their conscience and the Order, I begin
> to wonder whether it is worth a penny listening to them any
> longer.
>
> (*No Heaven for the Priest,* Enugu, February 1971, p.2.)

This pamphlet then goes on to criticize certain ideas about God and Christianity propagated by the clergy, especially the idea about God contained in the Old Testament. The author's conclusions are:

> I do not say there is no God. What I have tried to illustrate is that the God in the Old Testament of the Bible is not a true God. It is a god of confusion, a warrior, a murderer and a god interested in blood and sacrifices.
>
> This, certainly, is not that God of gods, the Almighty, Alpha and the Omega. Where this very God is, no one has been able to find out.

There was anger, scepticism and disillusionment in this first popular pamphlet to appear after the Nigerian war. Its mood is, as might well be expected, totally at variance with the mood of pamphlets which appeared before the war. Then, Christianity represented for the popular authors an anchor of security (only the intellectual authors were critical of its effect on Africans and the African tradition); after the war, a general mood of doubt and scepticism seems to have taken over. Popular authors, as reflectors of popular moods and attitudes, are likely to produce works that bear testimony to the realities of the moment.

Which is another way of saying that the anger and the disillusionment will pass. The reputation of the clergy has received a blow but Christianity itself has not been repudiated. The churches are as full as ever, though the 'spiritualist', African-based sects seem to have drawn away many converts from the older, cosmopolitan sects. What is most obvious in Igboland after the recent war is that people have become more critically aware of what religion should stand for in their lives. The old tendency to accept Christianity as one aspect of modern institutions is giving way to a deliberate choice of the religion or sect that brings most emotional, psychological and even material comfort. Numerous new sects are springing up and recruiting their followers from among the old, established sects. These are fighting hard to retain their dominance. New pamphlets which deal with the theme of religion will reflect this new reality.

10   Conclusion

Social change in modern West Africa is a complex phenomenon. There are specifically modern factors, among which must be reckoned modern education based on Western-oriented literacy, the modern economic, political and administrative institutions and the values and attitudes attaching to them, and the modern media of communication and mass information, all of which interact to produce the industrial civilization of the modern world. These factors, in Africa, overlie a traditional, agricultural base civilization, producing even greater complexity and flux than is evident where there has been a lineal development from a traditional to an industrial civilization. And yet it is possible, in spite of the flux and complexity, to disentangle the most vital elements in the modern African situation, to relate them to the whole body of cultural and social movements, and to see them as distinct aspects of the social and cultural experience.

One of the most important phenomena of the past twenty to thirty years in West Africa is the rising importance of the millions of literate men and women who have been swept into the modern world, and who assume a central role in the industrial system which is pressing the old rural–agrarian system of traditional Africa to the periphery of life and experience. The importance of this emergent, literate class does not depend on its size; for this class, though continually expanding, is still numerically small and marginal to the vast majority of peasants who can neither read nor write, and who inhabit the African villages. The significance of this emergent literate class lies in the responsiveness of its members to the needs of the modern state, needs which include the acquisition of new skills and techniques, new knowledge, new attitudes and outlooks. Moreover, the enthusiasm which the newly literate masses display towards the new industrial order and its values, and the volatile energy with which they operate the new system, has marked them out as the vanguard of industrial, technological civilization in West Africa. Not possessing the intellectual scepticism and inhibitions of the more thoroughly educated, the literate masses have become the most active agents and creative promoters of the industrial order.

Onitsha Market literature made its appearance at a time when this explosive release of mass energies and enthusiasm had already taken place as a result of the sweeping advances of education and modern industrialism. It became a medium for the celebration of this emergence of the masses, and their discovery of their potential in the building of a modern industrial culture in Africa. That is why the content of much of the popular pamphlets has the authenticity of an internal evidence; the writers and the subjects they deal with have a built-in intimacy of relationship. That is why the popular authors write with the commitment one encounters in the pamphlet literature: because they are dealing with situations of which they form a part, and about men and women with whom they have identity of views and attitude, and with whom they share identical responses to the modern situation. That is why also there is hardly any dissociation of writers from subjects, characters and situations.

The question sometimes raised in sophisticated, middle-class circles in Nigeria is whether the popular market pamphlets are literature at all, or whether they are mere entertainment. Related to this question, and probably deriving from it, is the tendency of the elite to treat popular writing with condescending tolerance and good-natured levity.

The question whether popular pamphlet writing is literature or entertainment arises from a narrow class snobbery and an equally narrow conception of literature. It is an over-easy sophistication which distinguishes between literature and entertainment in this arbitrary manner. Literature arises from man's inborn desire to create his own enjoyment and entertainment by drawing on the resources of language. The major defining features of literature necessarily include a conscious manipulation of words for the specific end of creating pleasure and enjoyment by exploiting the story-telling and dramatic propensities, as well as the poetical nature, of man. The raw material of literature is human experience which is put through the transforming 'sieve' of imagination. The end-product is fictionalized experience. The pleasure which a work of literature gives is thus based on how well the fictional world of literature mirrors the world of waking experience and also how successfully language has been utilized to produce desired effects, including the desire to confer pleasure and to entertain.

There is no doubt that the popular market pamphlets are literature; they satisfy our broadest expectations of works of literature. Their authors are keenly aware of linguistic implications; in fact, they are obsessed by the effects of language and the possibilities of language in the hands of creative artists. We have seen also that one of their main concerns is to provide entertainment, and that their works are enjoyed by the thousands of common readers at whom they are aimed. The source of their best effects is often the successful exploitation of linguistic potentialities. Also, the pamphlets sparkle with humour, their characters are full of vitality and the situations are full of exhilarating ironic twists and shrewd insights. Not even the most fastidious critic of the pamphlet literature will deny that it is full of vitality, that it is a store-house of humour and linguistic 'audacity' and a source of pleasurable entertainment.

A hostile middle-class commentator on the pamphlet literature once said in a review article in a Nigerian newspaper that she did not think much of the writing, but that whenever she was tired and bored with other activities, she would reach for a copy of an Onitsha pamphlet and then get so much entertainment from it that she soon recovered her strength and equanimity. This is a piece of unintentional praise which seems unwittingly to justify the claim of the pamphlet writing to be regarded as literature.

Pedants and purists have rejected the pamphlets' literary claims because of their crudities of expression and formal technique. But the pamphlet authors are not pedants. For all the linguistic crudities and formal weaknesses, the pamphlets throb with life and have fascinated and arrested the enthusiasm of thousands of common readers who have gone to them for entertainment, enjoyment and emotional stimulation. The example of Shakespeare shows that linguistic innovation does not harm the literary integrity of works of art. On the contrary, bold experiment with language may expand the linguistic dimension, bring a quality of freshness and sparkle, and heighten effect. Part of the creative prerogative of the artist is this right to create the linguistic world of his work. Our judgement rests on whether or not his experiment has served his intention well.

A more serious criticism of the popular market pamphlets is that they lack intellectual depth. This criticism is more difficult to repudiate. The pamphlet literature does not aspire to entertain and provide pleasure alone. One of its major preoccupations is also to provide instruction; in other words, to explore certain moral and intellectual territory, for the edification of readers. It is here that the weaknesses of the writing register most emphatically; the authors' intellectual limitations most clearly assert themselves in their diagnoses of social ills and their social prescriptions.

The point can be illustrated by comparison of the popular with the intellectual West African writers. Both groups are concerned to provide insights into contemporary West African life. They see things differently, largely because they deal with different areas of the common experiences they are exploring. The pamphlet authors concern themselves with surface appearances, while the intellectual authors look for underlying causes and explanations. Comparison of works by the two groups shows that in terms of their reflection of things as they actually are, we are likely to find the pamphleteers nearer to the experience of ordinary people than the sophisticated authors. They reflect the problems and crises of contemporary life in all their rawness. By the time these have undergone intellectual digestion in the works of the intellectual authors, a certain amount of blood must have been lost from the life that reappears.

But in the strength of the pamphlet literature also lies its weakness. Its spontaneity and freshness do not compensate for its lack of intellectual vigour. For good literature does more than reproduce the problems and crises of life. It should also show evidence of thought, evidence that the writer has wrestled with the problems before consolidating his insight. Literature should not only reproduce life, it should also point a way to fuller, better and more satisfying life; it should reveal the potentiality of life. Literature that fails to do this can appeal only to the unthinking section of the population. The pamphlet literature has been neglected by more sophisticated readers for this reason.

We are confronted in the pamphlets with the aggressive assertion of individualism. The claims of the individual are pressed in economic matters, in love affairs, in marriage and even in religious identification. All obstacles in the way of individual self-expression are impatiently pushed aside. The bearers of old-fashioned ideas which impede individualist fulfilment are quickly dismissed.

One may applaud the zeal and crusading vigour with which the pamphlet authors pursue individualism. But if we look for an expression of social awareness, of social responsibility and the values which promote social goals, we search in vain. Individualism without social responsibility leads inevitably to social parasitism, to preying on the social resources by individuals who do not themselves contribute anything substantial towards social progress.

It is in this area of social responsibility that the intellectual authors score over the pamphlet writers. The intellectual authors constantly link the fortunes of individuals to those of society at large. They tend to show that pursuit of individual goals without considering the effect on social well-being must undermine happiness and well-being at the individual level. These authors are therefore sceptical of the mere assertion of individualism.

It would be a mistake, of course, simply to dismiss the pamphlet authors by asking why their view of society has been so lacking in positive constructiveness, why the kind of morality they press has no root, and why their general attitudes have so little depth of emotional or intellectual conviction. The pamphlet authors are to a large extent victims of the modern commercially-provided media of entertainment, which themselves project individualism without social responsibility. We look at the commercial films which these popular authors and their audience watch night after night, and what do we see? We see a perpetual display of reckless individualism and lack of concern for social morality (as for example, in the glorification of the gangster hero). We find the corruption of basic emotions and appetites; violence and sexuality are confused and grossly stimulated, crime is glamourized, and material 'success' is elevated into a fetish. As for the newspapers and magazines directed at the common people, their pages are given to the same simple stimuli, which are reinforced by highly-coloured advertisements which appeal to related tastes. All these things have the effect of undermining social consciousness, of increasing antisocial individualism and of luring readers into shallow pleasures that corrupt the soul and impoverish the emotions. And what is most deplorable about this mass brutalization of taste and attitudes through modern media of entertainment is that it is done by proprietors whose sole interest is to make money.

What chance do the pamphlet authors have of seeing the problems of contemporary life clearly and constructively when their vision is obscured by the haze of inspired amorality engendered by modern commercial films, newspapers and magazines? The intellectual authors are able, by their superior intelligence and education, and their wider experience, to pierce through this haze and reveal the underlying realities as they affect individuals and society.

Many factors contribute to the making of a popular culture and the shaping of popular tastes. The kind of books available to the people in the early periods of their formal education, what they read thereafter, especially in their leisure hours, what kind of recreational facilities exist, the nature and quality of the organs of mass information which they patronize, all are crucial in the making of culture and in the fashioning of tastes. They should interest anyone who studies society and the evolution of cultural patterns and behaviour among these new literates. Those who plan educational programmes or are involved in the mass media, the controllers of the press, radio and television, and those who run the commercial periodicals, the cinema proprietors and commercial advertisers of all sorts carry a heavy responsibility in newly emergent states for promoting the health and development of popular culture.

Finally, any discussion of the Onitsha Market literature at this point in time must look forward to the future prospects. The recent Nigerian civil war hit the pamphlet literature hard. There was, in the first place, the upheaval which war normally brings, the disorganization of normal life, the displacement of populations, the destruction of the economic infra-structure and the unhinging of the security of the masses of the people. There was also devastation of the moral values of society, and psychological turbulence producing abundant harvests of spiritual anguish. Onitsha, the home of the pamphlet literature, was disturbed very early in the war and its magnificent market, the centre of the pamphleteering activity, was totally gutted. Many of the little presses from which the pamphlets issued were either destroyed or collapsed commercially.

The war hampered the continued production of the pamphlet literature, which had depended on an atmosphere of relative calm and optimism for its development. The war with its devastation and disorganization made it impossible for the popular authors to go on writing. A good many of them and their readers were on active war service and a number of them were killed or died from hardships resulting from the war. Chike Okonyia, for instance, one of the pioneers of the Onitsha literature and a witty story-teller, died during this period.

The psychological effect of the war also inhibited the production of the pamphlets. Post-world-war-two euphoria and the bright prospects held out to the masses by the new industrial order were important factors which stimulated the emergence of the pamphlet literature and conditioned the attitudes of the pamphlet authors. The effect of the Nigerian war was devastating. It destroyed the optimism, and sowed doubts and bitterness among the people. The bright prospects of the past yielded to gloom, death and disillusionment. The first post-civil-war pamphlet, Ogali A. Ogali's *No Heaven for the Priest,* reflects the mood of bitter disillusionment which replaced the pre-war mood of optimism.

With the revival of life in Onitsha, attempts have been made to restore the pamphlet literature. Those involved in the business side are hard at work re-establishing their trade. Old, battered copies of the pamphlets can be seen again on the racks in the makeshift markets all over the rehabilitated parts of Onitsha. The few surviving presses have begun to reprint a number of the pamphlet evergreens, usually at a much higher price than before the war.

Perhaps, one should not be too quick to pronounce the demise of the pamphlet literature. The power of the masses to revive after a major disaster should not be under-rated. The mood of bitterness and disillusionment may pass and yield place to a renewal of hope and an attempt to build more solid structures on the rubble of the past.

The more fundamental threat to the continued existence of the pamphlet literature may lie elsewhere. For some time, the book trade has been moving increasingly into paperback editions, with their lower prices. As long as the books dealt with subjects of no immediate or personal concern to the generality of local readers, they did not threaten the popular pamphlet market. But with the development by Heinemann of the African Writers series, and of the other publishers of cheap paperback editions, many of the readers who hitherto patronized the popular pamphlets are beginning to find in the paperbacks an alternative source of low-cost reading matter of equal relevance. In other words, one threat to the popular market literature is likely to come from editions of 'quality' works with a local interest. This threat will grow as local men enter the publishing business.

In another direction, the flourishing of cheap, romantic magazines, with their seductive photographs and sensational treatment of sex, has the effect of luring away some of those newly literate readers who previously patronized the market pamphlets. The proliferation of these sex-sensation periodicals, helped by wig-and-mini-skirt fashion-mongering, creates a cultural amnesia more crippling to the development of popular local creativity than the cheap paperbacks in the Heinemann Educational Books series.

The fate of the popular market literature of Onitsha hangs in the balance. If the people recover their shattered confidence, and begin to trust once more in a system which has brought them so much woe and near-destruction, if they successfully resist the bipolar seductions of the academic and the purple press, then they may yet survive as a vital creative force, making its own tastes, fashioning its own attitudes and giving authenticity to its own experience through the popular pamphlet literature.

Appendix

OUR
MODERN LADIES CHARACTERS TOWARDS BOYS.

THE MOST EXCITING NOVEL WITH LOVE LETTERS,
DRAMA, TELEGRAM AND CAMPAIGNS OF
MISS BEAUTY TO THE TEACHER
ASKING HIM TO MARRY HER.

"Hasty Climbers Have Sudden Falls"

BY

HIGHBRED MAXWELL

2|- Net

INTRODUCTION

OUR MODERN LADIES CHARACTERS TOW-
ARDS BOYS" is all about Miss Beauty and a
young teacher John Billy. It happened at that
time that Beauty fell in deep love with Billy and
she made every possible attempt to make Billy
marry her. It was all unfortunate for her as Billy
ignored her. Often and often she wrote love letters
to him on account of marriage. Billy replied
none of them and this arouse her and she went
in person to him. There she was received warmly
and she told Billy the purpose of her coming.
They agreed to marry themselves with the consent
of their parents. Within a short time after marriage disagreement arose between them because
the lady was not allowed to practice her formal
Job-Bar maid.

This brought about their divorce. At long
last Beauty repented, although it was medicine
after death. She, heart brokenly died a miserable
lonely and lamentable death. She died the worst
death as nobody mourned her.

FOREWARD

It is my conviction that authors are highly talented people and that good writers can be got from authors who have no degrees. The hand work of *Mr. Highbred Maxwell, a promising* scientific writer is a clear indication. In this invalueable book *"Our Modern Ladies Characters Towards Boys"* he has drawn the attention of the reading public to e v e r y day accurrence in human life. For this I recommend this book to you and your family. Don't miss a copy, have it and make it a kola to your visitors. They will enjoy it and will always remember you for it.

Read On.

OKENWA OLISHA

IMPORTANT NOTICE

The charaters in this book are purely imaginary and real names, both the dead or the living individuals were not intended to be mentioned, and if such be done it is accidental.

OUR MODERN LADIES CHARACTER
TOWARDS BOYS

Wife asked the husband to act as a passport for her.

By
Highbred Maxuwell,

ONITSHA.—NIGERIA.

CONTENTS

DIFFERENT OPINIONS

In this world, both men and women have different views in life. People have so many ways of scrambling to obtain money, by farming, trading, teaching, carpentary, ministry, tailoring and so many other hand works.

So many among our women can do a few of these occupations. So many of them who cannot do any of them have got another cunning ways of getting money. Similarly, many among them can change their minds when you are speaking to them about any other things, but when you are telling them anything concerning money, they keep their eyes open that they can see clearly as if with a telescope. It is true that money is the source and root of all evils, but its being the originator of all evils mainly affects our women.

They sight for money like a greedy dog longing for a piece of meat kept in a net near the fire side.

EYI—NNE—EYI—NNA

Now I comence with a story of one Miss "Eyi-nne Eyi-nna." This is a nickname adopted by MMA Ikeofor or Miss Beauty Ikeofor. Miss "Eyi nne Eyi-nna" means a lady without either the father's or the mother's characters. She was very beautiful with none to be compared with in the town of Isuochi in Okigwi division.

School Time:

When at school, she was doing well while she was in the primary classes. In the school, so many school boys and even some of the teachers loved Miss Beauty simply because of her beauty.

5

Among those that loved her, was one ugly fashionable teacher in another school This teacher gave the lady a false promise that after her standard six course, that he would marry her,

This promise made by the teacher, was pleasing to her because she had in mind that after her elementary course, she should expect a husband only from the teachers. The lady said nothing to the teacher's promise than "NO". I am to let you know that this "NO" of Miss Beauty does not actually come from her mind. She could only say within herself. "May God Bless these words".She forgot that she was a very beautiful lady whom the teacher thought should refuse to marry him. The teacher having learnt that she was pleased with the marriage proposal, started to make necessary arrangements to adopt her as a house wife.

He asked some of his friends to tell him their personal suggestions on such a proposal. Some of them advised him to further his studies and some told him to look for a certificated lady. Others discouraged him saying that the lady's beauty might perhaps be some bad lucks on his side.

After the instructions of his friends, he made up his mind to stop the proposal of engagement.

The lady's move:

Now the teacher's word to Miss Beauty disturbed her that she was not even settled. She waited to hear more from the teacher but all in vain. She even forgot that the final test which could determine her position was at hand. She did not study her lessons.

6

After some minutes consideration, she said to herself " I am to write a letter to that teacher, in that letter, I will inform him that I am waiting for him about what he told me last time.

She started the letter with good writing and grammar full of good English.

The letter reads;

Primary School Centre
Isuochi—Okigwi
19th Oct., 1959.

My dear Young Teacher,

I sieze this opportunity to inform you that I am waiting for you on account of what you told me last week. I should not have got the chance to inform you this because we are being worried from revision but owing to the blindness of love, I manage it so.

I wish to hear from you soon
Yours truely in love
Miss Beauty Ikeofor.

The teacher received the letter, read it over with curiosity and laughed. He laughed because he had changed his mind from the lady and was trying to give up the proposition. Further more he changed his mind because he thought that the lady could not accept the marriage proposal on account of her remarkable beauty, After reading the letter, he did not care to reply it nor did he worry to visit her but rather threw the letter into the waste paper basket.

The lady Miss Beauty waited for the reply to her letter but she could not see. This stipulated her to write a second letter in an inquiry of her first one.

7

Primaty School Centre
Isuocha-Okigwe
26th Oct., 1959.

My Dear Love,

I can not vividly imagine what has debarred you from replying my previous letter to you.

So as I have waited in vain, I write this second one rather with anxiety just to know your present opinion. I have every hope on you without any disappointment. My main purpose of writing this second one is to remind you about our enterprises. Have you forgotten that as far as beauty is concerned I have none to be compared with in the surrounding areas? Have you forgotten that I am popularly known as Miss Jive Correct?

Above all I am known as the proposed Beauty Miss for handsome men. I will show you that I am Miss Jive Correct in every service we undertake. I have refused so many young men who had approached me for this same purpose but to you, I accept yours assuming it to be your destiny. It will not please me if you happen to reject this destiny by giving a nagative reply. The best marriage you can get is that which love is the off spring and key note. I will give you more details when I write to you again.

I wish you happy days,
Yours in Love
Miss Beauty Ikeofor.

Having finshed this she despatched it to the teacher. When he (the teacher) received it, he read it with a loud hidious laughter and he wrote on the envelope in bold capital letters: "NOT TO BE REPLIED"

8

Beauty waited for the reply to her letter but all was hoping against hope. In a scattered mind, she thought within herself and said eargly: "After the final examination I will try again for it is said that if you try and don't succeed, try try try again". Therefore I must insist on this popular saying because it is not failure but low aim is crime and also remembering the friend at midnight............. I must try my possible best to win him over. At that time, the examination was at hand and within a short period it was all over. As soon as the examination was over, she said within herself, "Yes it is the preparation of the examination inconjuction with its fever and thoughts that deprived me from planning what steps to take about my engagement with that teacher. "Once I have not heard anything from him and have had no communication with him, I will better go directly to him and make this our first acquaintance." She set out in one bright sunny winter morning with thoughts of marriage and love scattered in her shallow troubled mind. She travelled through sand and stones and foggy, swampy deserted places where even the voice of an insect was not heard. Cannibals and wild flesh eating animals hunted her but she was delivered by the Almighty. Hardship was her's. No any kind of edible was purchased. She nearly died of hunger, thirst and loneliness. Lamentation was inevitable. The voice of concience blamed her and her mind was hanging on the weighing balance.

She bore all these hardships in pursuit of a husband. Yet she kept up courage as her affairs were critical, she determined therefore to find the way by the worst means.

9

After enduring all the troubles and dificultes on the way, she paved her way half dead into her destination.

On arriving, the teacher received her warmly. Trembling with fear and surprise, he told the lady that her letters were received though they deserved no reply. The lady was dead with shame as she had been humiliated. She laughed loudly i n comfort of herself. This was an assurance to her that the teacher had determined and decided not to marry her. So she went away sorrowfully though singing a comfortable song. When she was out of the gate, she said " What else can I do now as my engagement with the poor, dirty teacher had been totally broken? " Perhaps his not giving me any promising and favourable word may be because he was recently employed and he has not got any money in his pocket to maintain a wife" Concluding upon these facts, she thought it wise to write to him another letter which reads:-

St. Gabriel's School,
Ikeochi Town,
Okigwi Division,
28th Dec. 1959.

My Dearest Love.

Considering your performances towards my letters, I find out that your reasons are solid. It is obvious that your pocket is empty and the thought of marrying is at present out of question as means of maintainance is scarce. I am therefore to acertain you that once it is my utmost desire, money can not be the immediate blockade. For this particular purpose, expect me in your house on Saturday next for special arrangement.

10

May your thought concentrate on me,
I wish you happy dreams,
Lovely Yours,
Beauty Ikeofor.

When she finished the writing, she posted it to the teacher. When the teacher received it he opened it with eager curiousity. He was very pleased with the heading. This immediately changed his mind and he vowed never to leave her. He considered this chance to be his luck which would bring him great fortune. He instantly made provisions for the lady's arrival. He cleaned his rooms and decorated them and fortified them with electricity and electric fans. Radiogram was at his leasure. Meals prepared was beyond what he has been eating and for himself, he wore costly garments. Preparations made represents that made when expecting a respectable royal visit. It was all a fascinating sight.

` ARRIVAL OF MISS B. FOR ARRANGEMENT`:

On the evening of the appointed day, the beautiful, fashionable, well bred admirable lady arrived at the teacher's house. After the entertainment the teacher professed and addmitted before the lady that the contents of her last letter were all true. He said that his few months of employment has not fetched him enough money to enable him to maintain a wife, and so the thought of marriage was not in existence. She promised to bear the whole responsibility. More over she said that she should not allow her parents to demand from the teacher more than he could afford.

This was very pleasing to him and he gave the lady a solid promise that he should marry her. She then reminded him of her three names——

11

Miss Beauty, Miss Jive Correct, Proposed Miss Beauty for handsome men. The teacher was ignorant of the meanings of these names and neither did he care to know them he simply treated them lightly. After their timid conversations and having wished themselves happy dreams and good night, they departed to the separate rooms with a kiss. At dawn they woke and dinned with all kinds of drinks before any solid food was provided. While dinning, they hinted upon their previous night's conversation and all sanctioned it. After this the teacher escoted her beyond the gates and she traced her locus back.

ARRANGEMENT OF THE BRIDE PRICE

After some months, the teacher revealed his intensions to his parents. It pleased them though they feared that their son had not got enough money for that purpose. They asked him how much he has got in his pocket for his proposal. He told them ten pounds. This was not even sufficient for ordinary wine how much more other requirements" they said. He assured them that his intending wife promised to speak to her parents on account of this matter so that they might not expect much from him. On hearing this, they volunteered to give him (£15) fifteen pounds.

On that very spot, he told them that the payment of the dowery would be in the following week. They approved this and a day was set aside. John Billy (the teacher) instantly send a telegram to Beauty telling her the day of their coming to pay the bride price;—

Inland town Shool
Umuahia
30th Dec, 59.

Love:

Expect arrival payment of dowery January 5th 60, Billy.

12

Beauty and the parents made all necessary arrangements for their grand reception. Relatives were all invited. They killed two cows and five goats and all kinds of liquor were available. Food was in abundance, all were well prepared that everybody would eat to his/her satisfaction. Everything was ready for their reception and everybody was on the watch of their arrival.

DAY OF THE BRIDE PRICE

It was on a very gloomy rainy morning. As they set out, the weather was somewhat promising but having gone a quarter of the way shawers of rain fell, on their half way off, a heavy rain fell and they were drenched to the skin. They welcomed this as a luck "every disappointment is a blessing from God" was their chorus. Within a short interval they found their way to their inlaw's house. The people expressed their great sympathy because of the rain. This was followed by an introduction and serving of kola, after which the money was demanded.

They gave twenty gallons of palm wine and the sum of twenty five pounds. This was not satisfactory to their inlaws. They accepted this so far and demanded more fifty pounds in addition. After this, they were presented with their light refreshment, after which a short native dance was staged. At the end of the ceremony, the father of Beauty blessed her and her husband and gave her to him. All went home joyfully.

AT HOME

Not more than a month, the teacher's fears came to light. His wife has changed her promise

13

of supplying to consumption. Her demands were greater than their income. Even marriage was neglected and they lived contrary to the laws of the church because of inevitable poverty. Billy heard nothing than buy me this and that. He tried his best and bought all that could help her to maintain her ferminine beauty. She wasted all these within a few days and demanded the purchase of more. This arouse the indignation of her simple, loyal self made husband. Impatiently he asked her:-

Teacher   Why! what of those ones I bought the day before yesterday? Were they sold?

Beauty   Sold? What do you mean? women are known to be puppish. I must maintain my beauty by constant using of these things.

Billy   Please, try to use them economically as you know that we are as poor as the Church mouse.

Beauty   All right, I promise to use these ones economically if ever they are bought.

Billy   O well wife, I will go to the market and buy them for you tomorrow. These ones I will buy next, will last for the whole year if not, there will be no possibility o f buying any more.

Beauty   I support that. I am not in the least worried, any way that you think helpful is good.

Billy   Ah wife! I am going to the market to buy those things. My word is my bond expect them soon.

Beauty   Try therefore to get the best quality of each. (Billy goes to the market with great reluctance and bought the things required)

14

Beauty Alone; if ever he buys the ones that are not attractive and admired by men, I will undoubtedly reject them.

Billy Back from the market; Beauty! where are you, why do you not come out to bid me welcome? Any how it is a bye gone matter, come and have y o u articles.

Beauty (Runs out with a great speed that she nearly died of breath) Thank you very much these are certainly the ones I want.

Billy: I think t h a t I have performed your commissioned mission without misgive.

Beauty: It is true, thank you once more. I will now go and dress in my richest dress and go t o the "Wealthy Peoples Bar Hotel" for a dance is to be staged there to night.

Billy: Pardon! What do you say? going to dance? Is it not ridiculous and funny? you must as well serve in the bar. Any way I hope to go with you.

Beauty: Going with you? yourself o r another person. Ah! what do you mean by Miss Jive Correct. Have you ever danced or are you going today to learn?

Billy: Miss Jive Correct means that you are good in all jiving veriations. This name is one of the factors that urged me to marry you in that you will teach me to do the like.

Beauty: Don't mind for the present day because the arrangement of the days dance is

15

over. I have booked for some elegant youths who will dance with me.

Teacher: What? It is an absord, unusual, uncommon and unnatural, what do you intend? So I am going there to act as a passport for you, it is a public insult. Do you not know that when a woman is married, her movements is limited to her husband only, and her walking with any other person will be with her husband's personal permission.

Beauty: You are only proposing to marry me because nothing has been done to show that we have married, but what do you understand by proposed Beauty Miss for handsome men?

Teacher: Regard it not, it is only but a mere name because people can easily call you by any name they like.

Beauty It is not a mere name as you think it. Refering to my second letter to you, I made mention of the three names. Why didn't you think over them and understand or enquire for their separate meanings. So don't waste my time, the only concession for you is to peep through the window. Dancing with you will certainly low my prestige on the stage.

Teacher; Your going is strongly unwarranted or you insist and go and prepare to bear the consiquence. The penalty to this offence will bring you everlasting course and lamentation.

16

Beauty; I am ready to bear any penalty that is alloted to such an offence. I am going, anything may be the consiquence.

After so many disagreements and disputes, Miss Beauty went away with murmuring and anxiety to the hall. The husband's immediate great reaction was his deep thought in his inner room. He therefore decided to cancel his marriage with the lady. He feared that her names may in due time cause the worst calamity. He said that the whole arrangements would start immediately she was back. "I will order her to park to her parents." At 4 a.m. She came back to the annoyed teacher.

Teacher: Yes woman, you have satisfied yourself by mingling with harlots and associating with high way rubbers and womanizers. You have determined to go contrary to my s i n c e r e commands which will inevitably bring about our immediate divorce. Therefore may it please you to accept my writ of separation and quit from my house.

Beauty It is not your personal fault. You are free to address me in any abusive language that you think appropriate.

It is due to my intolerable mistake that I run to you. I was blinded with love on your behalf hence you are correct in your analysis of my character. Weighing your comparison of my character with a prostitute will surely bring d o o m to my public life. This is an insult to my highly dignified parents. It must undoubtely be reported to them

17

Teacher: To be sure; your manners and public performances do not actually show that you should live with a husband. So it is better for y o u to pack and go back to your parents so that you may be free to act as you like if ever they will justify your attitudes. Tell them that I shall come to take back my money.

Beauty Demaning your money does not affect my daily life The amount you paid is very small to be mentioned. One will be very ashamed to say that he married a wife with only twenty five pounds. I promise you, your hot incorrect, bloody money collected with conspirancy will not be put into our honest bag; so the money is at present laying at the door waiting for you to come and take it.

DIVORCE

After all these bitter quarrellings. In the following morning Billy took his wife (Beauty) and hesitated to his inlaw for his proposed divorce. On their arrival the cause of their arrival was instantly understood by their gloomy heavy angered countenance. As guests, they were received well but they took everything with heavy hearted The inlaw at once asked Billy to tell him how they were living. Billy related the incident with noble tears keeping nothing back. He told them how his wife left his house for a dance in the bar without his sanction.

18

My wife, he said left the house upon all my insistence to debare her from going and more over her late arrival at home, roused my utter indignation. Please I beg to go in order to give her chance to tell you all if I have lied. She has persuaded me to marry at this early year and has also brought about our separation which is my utmost desire.

Inlaw: " This is a very small matter to separate you. I therefore appeal for peace and beg you to settle it. Disputes and quarrels often arise between husband and wife yet they are all the test for love; If ever they fail to settle it, it proves that their love has not tap root and strong foundation and is built not upon the rock but upon sand where anti winds will blow them aside. If this is on your part, it means that you are all objects of caricature, but remember; " prevention is better than cure " Forget every misbehavour and misconduct and live together with happiness so that you will be source of envy to your mates. Take her therefore I give you dominion over her."

Billy   Thank you for your noble wise advice but I fear that I can't act contrary to my will. There is no power under heaven that can convince me, so I have decided to leave her

Beauty Father, don't trouble yourself. He is below the standard of my choice. There is nothing again to unite us. I can not again afford to bear the burden of humiliation in his antique old fashioned residence.

19

There are many other churches besides St. Gregory's, perhaps my luck awaits me on a modest well bred, fashionable gentleman. I have refused the hands of so many wealthy intellectual people therefore lets forget the question of husband and wife. "How con I be in the fire of hell while I am still on earth. Please tell him to quit my sight and paddle his own canoe or I insult him to the last degree. He is unable to provide me with my needs. He is a parasite, a pamper, a sadist, indigent, he is a scoundrel, he is harsh and hasty of temper mingled with ignorance. He is rather barbarous. Oh! I can scarcely venture to qualify him. Tell him to go at once or I order the boys to drive him out.

Billy: She is perfectly correct with her analysis of my character and her description of my residence yet I am only demanding my money to see if I can make up.

Inlaw: Do not be heavy hearted take it cooly my dear, it is always so. Bear it and dispute it like a man, girls are very insolence. I promise to give you your money whenever she is married to another man.

With this, Billy went home nearly half dead as he had been mortified and humiliated. As soon as he was out of the gate, his Inlaw was moved with pity about his bitter departure, With anger, he asked his daughter Beauty to tell him the cause of their departure without any previous information.

Beauty The only trouble between us is all about Jive Correct, Miss Beauty and proposed Beauty for handsome men, besides these there is no other cause. He was angry because of my attending to a dance and also of my asking for things that should help me to maintain my regular beauty, and more over for seeing me dancing with my boy pets.

Father Even so far you are wrong and must apologize. A married somebody as you are is under the entire control of the husband and must also be loyal and faithful together with obedience to him, but you have acted on the contrary.

Beauty Father, you know that I must always act to the meanings of my name. As Miss Jive Correct, I must Jive with any near by fellow, as Beauty I must use all kinds of powders and pomade to maintain my beauty. Proposed Beauty for handsome men when shows that I am not a wife to him alone. He was aware of these names yet he married me but would not allow me to keep to their meanings. I am not so much wrong if at all I am.

Father Even though You are still wrong. I did not give you any of these mentioned assuming names. You have crowned your self with odd names which will bring your down-fall. You have insulted the kind humble youth, uttered all amount of nonesense against him and refuse to apologize. It will react upon you and you must reap it.

21

Beauty from that moment began to have feelings of endurable punishment: She instead of receiving blessing from the father, was crowned with everlasting curse. All the time, she lived with her parents nobody else asked of her. The names which she gave to herself brought about her doom and loneliness, because they were folded with trapping meanings. She was known throughout the division because she visited every theatre and halls. She contacted with both good and bad and her general respect was lost. Her beauty after all come to nothing since none know that she was in existence. All the honourable personalities, boy pets and her dancing comrades deserted her and her state was a funny one and lesson to the public.

Repents:

Not so long from this state, she came to the reliazation of her past performances. Casting a retrospective glance over her past attitudes towards her divorced husband, she was convinced that she deserved nothing but death. She cried and lamented to the last degree yet nobody paid a heed to her. She therefore desired immediate death and raised an alarm of cry to the Almighty, when she saw that nothing remained for her-

All Things Are Taken From Me.
"What Is It That Will Last?
'What Pleasure Can I Have To War With Father ?
Why Should I Toil Alone, and Make Perpetuals Still From One Sorrow To Another Thrown.

22

There Is No Joy But Calm !
Why Should I Only Toil, the Roof And
Crown Of Things.·
All Things Have Rest And Ripen Towards
The Growl.
Give me Long Rest Or Death, dark Death
Or Dreamful Ease."

Consequence:

Lamentation and dreadful thoughts drove the beautiful lady to madness what else? She was left unattended, no treatment was given to her and she died lonely and miserably. She died unmourned either by the parents or by the public.

Conclusion:

The divorce between Miss Beauty and John Billy will be an example to our women. They should learn to be obedience, faithful, loyal, servicable and charm so that they may be sources of pride to their husbands least they may be subjected to servitude. If Beauty had been quiet, rectitude, polite and humble. she should have lived with Billy peacefully. From Beauty, women should avoid to be haughty, querulous, recusant, rampart and refractory because these are the off springs of pomposity. Beauty forgot the words of the Bible which says "Thou shalt be subject to thy husband and he shall have dominion over thee" Having forgotten t h i s, she thought of governing her husband which never happend anywhere.

When this was gone, Billy married a beautiful certificated lady. They lived happily for all the time and people imitiated them. Beauty lost her opportunity and never gained it.

HIGHBRED MAXWELL,

The Author of this Novel is also the Sole

Publisher of

MONEY PALAVAR

and the agent of so many Novels.

HIGHBRED MAXWELL'S BOOKS

(1.)   *The Gentle Giant*
(2.) *Out Modern Ladies Characters Toward Boys*
(3.)   *"Don't Forget Me"* (*In Preparation*)
(4.) *"Wonders Shall Never End"* (*In Preparation*)
(5.)   *Money Palaver*
(6.)   *£9000,000,000 Man Still Says No Money*
                (*In Preparation*)

Order your copies from
THE STUDENTS OWN BOOKSHOP,
17, Bright Street,
ONITSHA.

ELIZABETH
MY
LOVER

A Drama

"LOVE WORKS WONDERS"

Printed by All Star Printers, 62 Iweka Road, Onitsha.

ELIZABETH

MY

LOVER

A Drama

By

Okenwa Olisah

Obtainable From:-

A. ONWUDIWE & SONS,
R 9 No. 6 Onitsha Main Market,
P. O. Box 214,
ONITSHA—NIGERIA.

2/6d Net Price.

PREFACE

This romantic play,' Elizabeth my Lover' is an interesting drama inteded to amuse the Reader and keep him happy all times. It entertains you at your leisure hours and demonstrates before you the work of love. It is my hope that spectators will enjoy the play when staged.

For your information, all the statements and activities attribution to the people in this pamphlet, is purely an imaginary work. But this dosen't touch or affect the lesson which you may learn from this work. Take note as from now that LOVE works wonders, and that it is not allthat easy, to separate two sweethearts who are in deep love, or impose a husband on a girl who dosen't like the man.

Read on and bear in mind that to love is one thing and to maintain the love, is another thing.

OKENWA O LISAH
(The Author)
And the Strong Man of the pen.

CHA   OF THE PLAY

ELIZABETH=   The lover of Mr. Ototofioko

Mr. OTOTOFIOKO— The lover oi Elizabeth

CHIEF COOKEY=   The Father of Elizabeth

CECELIA— The Mother of Elizabeth

MADAM OLIAKU= Chief Cookey's Neighbour

CHIEF JAJA= Who woefully failed to get Elizabeth

BELGAN— Who throws a cocktail party

MASTER OF CEREMONY

CHAIRMAN

ATTENDANTS

GUESTS

HOTEL MANAGER

IN CHIEF COOKEY'S PALOR

(ENTER ELIZABETH AND OTOTOFIOKO)

ELíZABETH: My sweetheart Mr. Ototofioko, I wish to speak to you now from the bottom of my heart. From the abundance of heart the mouth speaketh. I love you with all my heart and so I can't hide anything for you. You are mine and I am yours, no different. Where your live is my home and where you die is my grave. I can't do without you and anything that happens to you directly happens to me because love is wonderful.

You may agree with me that love works wonders. It can kill and can save. It is influencial. Love is a worm affection and a wonderful thing. It is deep and counts no erros. It is blind. Love highly contributes to happiness which makes life up-to-date and enjoyable. Making friendship or marriage without love is rather just like eating a food without salt. You can't beat love, it is influencial. My darling Ototofioko, It seems that you are anxious to know why I am very tiny and unhappy these days?

OTOFIOKO: First of all my dear, let me agree with you that love works wonders. It can make and unmake. I am very interested with the statements made by you in con ection with love. It is 100 percent. My dear Elizabeth, you may agree with me also that no fire without smoke. I believe that something might have caused you to comment about love affairs. May it please you to tell me the cause. And again, it is within my anxiousness to know why you appear very tiny, uncheerful and unhappy nowadays. Your weak appearance these days causes me a great deal of unhappiness and mental sickness.

ELIZABETH: Something is wrong. Our lives are no longer in safety. The thing is very heavy in my mouth to say out, but unavoidably I must say it: You see, my old father Chief Cookey, has been looking for you every where to shoot you to death. He also threatened to kill me unless I boycott you. He is madly against our friendship. He has the support of the entire members of the family excepting my mother who wants us to carry on with out love deals.

I have advised my father through my mother never to carry out his threats otherwise the law deals with him. I see no reason why he will kill us because we love ourselves. Love making is not a strange news, it is welcomed. My sweethart, Mr. Ototofioko if my father wants to murder us because we naturally love ourselves, he can do so. I am ready even now to die for your sake.

6

OTOTOFIOKO: Oh Elizabeth my lover! Elizabeth my lover!! My haed scatters, my head scatters, my head scatters. What is all these nonsence! That your old father who had played his youth is trying to disturb us. He cannot succeed because our love is so deep now that it is not breakable. Your dad is making a grave mistake, unpardonable one.

He say that he will be killing us. Well if he thinks it right, he may execute his plans. The Government will hold him responsible. We have committed no crime. Love is commonly played every where. My darling, I suggest that I write to him in a good way. In the letter, I will not be offensive just to ask him to refrain from what he is thinking about us as there is no harm, danger or bad thing in our being lovers. I will recall him to his youthful days and inform him that both of us are prepared at any time to die together as far as love is concerned

ELIZABETH: Mr. Ototofiioko, my sweetheart. There is no need to pen my father. He cannot read or write. Your letter to him will only add insult to injury. Leave him to do his worst. I don't care any hell. If I am murdered simply because I love you,

7

I am okey. I am only sorry for your own lief, as for me I am not worried. Let the worst happen.

OTOTOFIOKO: My darling, the situation is critical and we are in temptatin. We should know what to do otherwise we get it hot. Your dad, Chief Cookey, does not joke. He is serious and can kill us. I have seen some fathers who had taken a similer action.
I hope your mother can help to bring your dad to order. As a wife she has a part to play in suppressing the anger of your dad. Therefore you can tell your mother to take action now when it is not late.

ELIZABETH: It seems you are afraid. I cannot blame you for life is precious. I cannot disagree to tell my mother to take action for your sake, as for me I have chosen to perish.

OTOTOFIOKO: It will be wise darling, if you tell your mother to meet your father and speak to him. It does not mean that if your father persists to be against our love making that we would cease to go on. This will never happen. Should he persist to be against our friendship, we can meet again and know what to do.

ELIZABETH: Okay my dear, I have heard what you said. Please move away with run, see my dad returning from farm with a big stick, if he meets us here, certainly he beats us to death with the stick. He is annoyed, he is always annoyed especially by this time he is in loggerhead with me.

OTOTOFOKO: Okay. Thank God you see him in time. (he runs away through the back yard and Elizabeth runs inside the room)

ENTER CHIEF COOKEY

CHIEF COOKEY: (*he calls*) Elibeth! Elibeth! Elibeth-ie!

ELIZABETH: Sir (*She comes out at the palour*)

CHIEF COOKEY: Elibeth! Elibeth! My palour dirty you no washing it with broom. We tin you dey do since morning. You no folloxing me go farm. You stay for house and you no fit do any home work. You no be better person. The day way I go beatam you, you go die that day. Govement no go asking me any thing.

Some time you don go for house of that thief thief boy wey you dey callam Otofioko. That boy wey dey deceive you. Him grade don marry since but he dey still make love love with you. I don say I go kill you people with my gun. You wan make useless. Not for my eye dan one go happen.

9

ELIZABETH: Let me refer you to the dirtiness of the palour, it is my duty to sweet it without being told, but the broom I should have use was locked in. I searched for the key to open the door but I could not see it.

Coming to the question of my friendship with Mr. Ototofioko, it is worong to refer him as a "thief thief boy". This damages his reputation. He is a gentleman of no equal. Know this now or never.

CHIEF COOKEY: Who you dey talk to like dis? Me your father wey born you and dey feeding you. I go beatam you now, you die for Ototofioko trouble. (*Chief Cookey holds Elizabet and begins to beat*)

ELIZABETH: (*Crying*) Mama! Mama! Mama! come and save me, I die

CECELIA: (Comes out from the kitchen and shouts) "You want to kill? You want to kill?" She holds Chief Cookey to allow Elizabeth run away to save her from further punishment. Elizabeth runs away, and Chief Cookey turns to beat his wife, and a free fight takes place.

ENTER A NEIGHBOUR

A neighbour Madam Oliaku hearing some noise comes in to stop the fight between Chief Cookey and his wife Cecelia.

OLIAKU: Neighbour stop fighting, this is regrettable and childish. (She separates the fighters). Neighbour what is all this trouble? Please don't fight again.

CHIEF COOKEY: Neighbour I go fighting, again this bad wife and her daughter wanting to killam me because of one thief thief boy Ototofioko, a drunkard. Elibeth and his mother don pass me in this house. My word no reach penny again. Them go see "ugbalugba case."

I tellam Elibeth make she marry but she refuse and saying she go making love with Otofioko. Neigbour this na good thing? You tell your daughter say make she marriage and she saying no, that she go make love love. This no go happen for this my two eyes.

Elibeth my daughter no dey hear my word again since she starting to make love love with Otofioko, a drunkard and thief thief boy. When I tell Elibeth say leave Otofioko, she begin to abusing me. I warn Otofioko say no come my house again but when I go farm, he come and begin to dancing with Elibeth. "Which kan trouble be dis?"

OLIAKU: Cecelia what do you say about this?

CECELIA: Don't mind him. He can say what ever that comes out of his mouth. He is fond of lies, distortion and unbecoming words.

11

CHIEF COOKEY: Neighbour hear now Misisi dey address me badly. I go fight again. She go see "ugbalugba" case now. I meanam.

OLIAKU: Neighbour don't mind her, you know how we woman talk.

CECILIA: To continue what I am telling you, I was in the kitchen busy cooking when I heard my daughter crying like a person held by a tiger. I ran in and met her father beating her mercilessly. What I did was to make it possible for Elzabeth to run away in order to save her from further punishment. My husband then turned to fight me.

I have advised him as a wife to leave Elizabeth and Ototofioko alone. They can carry on with their friendship. I see no harm in it. Elizabeth and Ototofioko are of age and deeply love themselves. He has threatened to kill Elzabeth and Ototofioko. Is this right?

OLIAKU: Love affairs cannot invite a trouble or fighting in a family. I have several daughters and I know how I train them. I restrict their movements to certain extents. My eldest daughter has a lover. I don't approve it, however I have not told my daughter to leave the boy. I leave them to play their time as I did during my days.

On the other hand, Cecelia, your husband may have his good reasons to object to your daughter's friendship with Mr. Ototofioko whom he describe as a thief and a drunkard.

I cannot allow my daughter to be in amicable terms with a boy of a questionable character. So review your support for your daughter's friendship with Ototofioko.

CECELIA: Madam Oliaku, please take note that Mr. Ototofioko is neither a thief nor a drunkard. The boy is good. My husband has intentionaly painted him black.

CHIEF COOKEY: No minam neighbour, the boy is thief thief bóy and a drunkarding. Na hooligan.

OLIAKU: What I want to say before going away as a stranger is waiting me, don't quarrel or fiight again. A problem is not solved in this way. All of you should cool down and go to rest first.

CHIEF COOKEY: Good neighbour thankio. I gree the thing wey you say. I no go fighting again. Only my misisi and my daughter dey make wisdom for me, this na motor "tailboard wisdom."

OLIAKU: Okay I move out, live in harmony.

(*Exit Madam Oliaku, and Chief Cookey, has wife and daughter go to rest*).

CURTAIN FALLS.

13

SCENE 11

IN OTOTOFIOKO'S ROOM

Two months later Elizabeth's love with Ototofioko becomes deeper "than ever." Elizabeth and Ototofioko sit in Ototofioko's room to discuss the trouble which falls upon their love.

ELIZABETH: My sweetheart, you might have heard that my father beat me for your sake. He also fought with my mother. Things have not been quiet in my family. My father has extended his threats to my dear mother. He said that he will murder three of us unless I separate with you. As you either said, my father does not joke with this matter. He alleged that you are a thief, a drunkard and a hooligan. I and my mother have denied these charges.

I have come for us to discuss current events now and know what to do for there is really trouble. No day that my father will not quarel with my mother with regards to our deep friendship.

OTOTOFIOKO: (*Shaking his head*) My heart was burning and sorrows were mine the day the regretable news of the fighting was broken

14

to me. I heard that your father beat you mercilessly merely because we love our selves. The whole incidents were made known to me by a male friend of mine who who lives near your house.

You have suffered for my sake. Please my sweetheart don't feel it too much. I hope that after long run that we will conquer this temptation for "things are not what they seem and life is but an empty dream" I hope that time will come when your

father will come to know that he is fighting against nature. I pray that God may do wonderful work for us—to change the mind of your father.

I am of the opinion that your father's worst disease is his illiteracy. Being that he is not educated as to be able to read some novels to know about the work of love, what it means and its strenght, be foolishly opposes our friendship.

He has alleged that I am a thief, a drunkared and a hooligan. He said this deliberately to spoil my famous name.

As your father is against our *love making*. I will come to him to marry you. This is marriage and under the law of the First, Order, he has no right to say NO.

15

ELIZABETH: My swertheart, I am over happy now. May God do His will. I will be the happiest person on earth when we become husband and wife. The Nigerian Law makes it illegal for a father to oppose a consented marriage of his daughter and her intendings. Therefore come to meet him tomorrow. Don't waste time.

OTOTOFIOKO: Okay darling, I will be coming to-morrow's evening, tell your mother. You can go now, the night is coming.

ELIZABETH: Before going, please let us kiss for our kissing makes me to forget my sorrows. *(They kiss)*

EXIT ELiZABETH

CURTAIN FALLS

SCENE 111

IN CECELIA'S BED ROOM

ELIZAETH: Mama for your information, my lover Mr. Ototofioko working under the Ministry of Communications and Aviation, will be coming tomorrow to marry me. Please support the m a r r i a g e.

CECELIA: My daughter, I will support but I am afraid that your father will not agree. He hates that boy Ototofioko. He dosen't want to see him at all. However, we wait to hear what your dad will say tomorrow when Ototofioko comes.

ELIZABETH: One thing must happen if he refuses: I must follow Mr. Ototofioko go for I love him to the salvation of my soul.

CECELIA: My daughter you cannot follow him like that.

ELIZABETH: Untill tomorrow you see what will happen.

Cecelia Let everything be tomorrow but you should act reasonably.

ELIZABETH Okay.

Both Cecelia and Elizabeth quit the bedroom.

CURTAIN FALLS

SCENE V

IN CHIEF COOKEY'S PALOUR

Enter Ototofioko and his brothers

17

CHIEF COOKEY: This thief thief boy Otofioko, wettin you dey finding for my house. Go away quickly quickly. I go call police for you.

OTOTOFIOKO: There is nothing bad in my coming here, Chief Cookey. May it please you to hear that I come to marry your daughter Elizabeth.

CHIEF COOKEY: Bush boy, hooligan, thief thief boy and drunkard. You no go marry my daughter. You no having money. I don see the big man wee go marriam. So go, I go beatam you with my walking stick.

CECILIA This is never in the list the way to treat somebody. It is offensive to refer Ototofioto as a thief, hooligan and a drunkard. He is not. Under no circumstances will you beat a person who comes to marry your daughter. Take note of this. I am in support of the marriage.

CHIEF COOKEY: Big woman, my master, I dey hear you. You want fighting again and you go see trouble run away. You don enter into arrangement with Otofioko, thankio. You go see with your eyes.

Otofioko go. I dey tell you now with clear eyes. The time wee I go vex, you will see paraver. I no love you the person wee I love go marry my daughter, you hear.?

18

ELIZABETH: Papa, I wonder why you have been going astray as far as my good terms with Ototofioko is concerned. You cannot, under the fundamental human right choose a husband for me. This is my entire right. You cannot also impose a husband on me. If you refuse my marriage with him, well be informed that I wil go with him, whether you like it or not. So answer Mr. Ototofioko in a favourable tone.

CH. COOKEY'. Elizabeth I go beat you again. No talk again Otofioko no go marry you. Na Chief Jaja go marry you. Na my friend for long long time. He getting money plenty and go pay me £250.

JAJA: I am a big chief, Elizabeth, I go pay any amount your father charging me. This boy Otofioko is poor. He no get money.

ELIZABETH: Chief Jaja, my seeing you here annoys me. Please go with your money. If you like pay £1,000 to my father. You are not paying it on my head.

CH. COOKEY: Chief Jaja pay me £250 I go forcam marry you. Na my daughter, na me bornam. Na nonsense ide talk.

CECELIA: You must change with the time. This time is no longer the olden days when fathers forced their daughters to marry "contrary to their wishes "

19

CHIEF COOKEY: Na me dey control this house, whatever I decide na final.

OTOTOFIOKO: Chief Cookey, I cannot insult you as you have done to me. Be it known to you that under the law of the First Order you have no right to refuse my marriage with your daughter. You have no right also to impose a husband on her. So take my £30, the lawful bride price.

CHIEF COOKEY: You are a beast, if you no go away now I shoot you with my gun. Why not marry my daughter for 1d. I no blame you, because you never born, you no know the suffer wee dey for borning a child. Na yim make you dey talk nonsense. Monkey like you.

ELIZABETH: Papa, you have seriously offended me and Ototofioko. Don't fight against nature. Nothing on earth stops my marriage with Mr. Ototofioko. If you like, purchase ten more guns. Whether you like it or not I must follow Ototofioko go today other I die. I love Mr. Ototofioko deeply and cannot be happy without him.

I love all the parts of his body. He is a gentleman of no equal, know this now or never. He has personality. He is handsome, healthy, cultured and educated. You can t beat him—unbeatable. He is my taste and what are you talking!

20

My sweetheart Mr. Ototofioko is working under the Ministry of Communications and Aviation. He holds an important post but you are calling him hooligan. Dessit from insulting and using unbecoming words against him. Never mar his famous name.

CECLIA: Elizabeth my daughter talk less, you are addressing your dad. My own is that you can marry Ototofioko.
   He cannot compel to marrry this old, illiterate Chief Jaja with dirty teeth and dirty clothes. Your right must be respected.

CHIEF COOKEY: I am annoyed, I go fiight now ebery body go away. Ototofioko go. Misisi go, go in with your daughter . I dey annoyed Chief Jaja go, tomorrow come back. You must marry my daughter. My word is final. Na me de control this house. God forbid, woman no go control me.

CHIEF JAJA: Okay Chief Cookey, I go come tomorrow with £500. Thankio Chief.

(EXIT CHIEF JAJA.)

CHIEF COOKEY: Otofioko go now now. You go see trouble now. (Chief Cookey gets hold of his big walking-stick and begins to flog Mr. Ototofiokow and Elizabeth. Mr. Ototofioko runs aay with his sweetheart

21

Elizabeth. Mr. Ototofioko's brothers also leave the parlour to go for Chief Cookev is angry).

CURTAIN FALLS

SCENE V

Mr. Ototofioko is livving with Elizabeth since three months without paying a brass farthing, because Chief Cookey bluntly refused the thirty pounds and the marriage. Elizabeth and Ototofioko discuss the situation.

OTOTOFIOKO: My dear, some people are forming bad opinion against us. These are unwise people. Your father, Chief Cookey, is very angry now. He has been sending me warnings through many people and threatening to finish my life unless I send you back to him in order to sell you to Chief Jaja, grade one illiterate.

I have told your father through those he sent to me, that if he is ready now to accept the £30, that I will send it to him at once but if he cannot accept it, well I cannot do ortherwise. He will either sue me or carry out his fatal threats.

22

ELIZABETH: My dear, your message to him is appreciated. If he likes, let him take the £30 or do his worst.

I will never go to marry Chief Jaja. I don't love him and my father cannot impose him on me. Chief Jaja has plenty money but he never attract me. I dislike him too much. He never wash. His teeth are decayed and his clothes are always dirty. How can I marry this type of bushman of the olden days. God forbid!

OTOTOFIOKO: One thing I heard again is this: you father has told one person to tell me that under the native law and custom that if we bear any child that it belongs to him hence he has not accepted any bride price from me. This is possible in Iboland and therefore I will post the £30 to him or pay it to him through the treasury.

ELIZABETH: It is true he can claim the child, so register the £30 to him or pay it through the treasury. Do this to-day.

OTOTOFIOKO: One thing is regrettable now, the £30 is not complete. It remains £6 to complete it. Oh what will I do?

ELIZABETH: My dear don't worry yourself. I have up to £9 here. I will give you the £6 to complete it. If you need the whole £9, this can be given to you.

OTOTOFIOKO What a love my dear! give me the £6 and keep the remaining £3, I may need this next time.

Elizabeth gives him the £6

Thank you very much my dear. May God give us long life, to enjoy the love between us. I must never in life forget this £6 you gave to me. It gives me a very big impression. It is a step towards a succesful marriage and an evidence that a good house wife can help her husband when in difficulty.

My dear I know that you love me to the last and can do anything to please me. You have been displeasing yourself inorder to please me.

You followed me without paying a brass farthing on your head, though I paid your father £30 but he refused but you never mind that he refused it and you followed me inspite of his threats.

24

ELIZABETH: My dear, yes I followed you freely because love works wonders. It can do anything bad or good. I have told you time with out number that I love you more than any other person on earth. I love you even more than my very mother who born me. Just immagine the strenght of the love.

The more I see you, the more I love you. The more I hear about my father and Chief Jaja those against us, the more I will be annoyed. Chief Jaia, the old man of the olden days cannot buy me with money. If he likes let him offer me £10,000 I must never accept it —£10,000 my "Yatsh!" I have no regard for Chief Jaja's money. My regard go to love. I am not Mr. "Judas" who loves money more than his very life.

My dear let me tell you one short story. As I was going to the market yesterday to purchase some food stuffs, I met one tall man on the street who dressed like a gentleman. He called me Elizabeth I never turned to him or answered and I kept on going to my very direction leaving my back to answer him whatever he may talk.

25

This man repeated calling me and telling me to disappoint you and go back to my father's house. He said you are poor and that you are his junior in the Ministry of Comminications and Aviation. Still I never talked to him and going to the market steady. I knew he was jealousing you and nothing more. This bush man followed me to the market and it was there that I warned his seriously to go away with his satan other wise he got it hot and he went away with shame.

OTOTOFIOKO: My dear you are an ideal lover. I am convinced that you never love my riches but my person. You have reacted to that bush man in the way he deserved it. Some people are jealousing me because I am in love with a girl of your calibra. If they like, let them hang because I am in love with you.

That unknown bushman thought that when he told you that I am poor and his jonior in the Ministry of Communications Aviation, that this would make you to dislike me not knowing that you are not worried whether I have money or not because rich men had approached you for marriage and you denounced them.

My dear, I thank you for your reaction
to that beast who pretended that he is working uuder the Ministry of Communications
and Aviation. A vagabond like him. I must
never forget "man is a jealous being;
man is an enemy to man."

Since "man is an enemy to man I am afraid nowadays
as to whom I can trust. I have trusted so many men to
my sorrows, friends today enemies tomorrow.
Man does not want the goodness and progress of the
other man.
Man is envious, greedy, selfish, wicked, dangerous
and unreliable.
Man wants the downfall of the other man.
Man makes man wicked.
Man is a devil to man.
Man is a trouble to man.
Man is a bad luck to man.
Man is an obstacle to man.

My dear, you might be surprised to hear
me spoke against my sex. The spirit of
God in me had made me voice those
words for man has faults.

ELIZABETH: Darling, I was touched by those words.
You are an orator. What you said are facts.
I cannot forget the unbecoming statement
made by one man last week. He
told me at a public place that my love
to you is a disgrace to me. He

warned me to give up my love for you and
said that you are of a junior class of
people. So I agree that "man is an enemy
to man."

Man can do anything to man. Man is
Satanic. Man has no love for his fellow
man. Man hates man. Man easily does bad
things but hardly do good things.

My darling, we leave the people of the
world with their faults for God shall judge
all souls. Send that £30 to my dad today
and tell him that we shall wed in few weeks
time. The holy wedlock must come to pass
whether he likes it or not.

OTOTOFIOKO: You see my dear, I shall once more
try to approach your father for peaceful
atmosphere. I have forgotten the stick he
flogged us.

Let us endure it. Your father is an old
man and we can tolerate some of his weak
points where possible. We will meet him
tomorrow with the thirty pounds. I will
advice him to support our marriage and
accept the BRIDE PRICE. We shall pray
so that God may change his mind and he
agrees. I Will like him to bless our marriage.

28

ELIZABETH: My dear, I have no objection in our meeting him tomorrow.

OTOTOFIOKO: My dear we have spoken a lot. I am tired. Let's go to sleep and rest for we would not die before our deaths.

(THEY GO IN TO SLEEP)

CURTAIN FALLS

SCENE VI

IN CHIEF COOKEY'S PALOUR

(*Enter Elizabeth and Mr. Ototofioko and they meet the old man drinking a big bottle of illicit jin. Cecelia is present.*)

OTOTOFIOKO: Chief, good evening Sir.

CHIEF COOKEY: Me no want your salutation. You don kam again to insulting me?

OTOTOFOKO: Never, I come to make peace with you. If I have done any wrong to you, forget and forgive me. To err is

29

human, to forgive is divine. I never have in mind to offend you. It all apear that you misunderstand how things go these days

I have the £30 with me here. Please accept it with all pleasure.

CHIEF COOKEY: I no go takam itu small. I marry this my wife £250. You think say I be fool to marriam £250? You take my daughter go since. You no fear. Your head no correct.

ELIZABETH: Papa, take the £30. It is good. Anything above it means selling me.

CECELIA: Just accept the £30. As a Chief, you would not creat the impression that you want to become rich with your daughter. Things are got cheaper from wealthy people. A poor man goes to a big man for help and support. If you can care to take my advine, forget whatever amount Chief Jaja may give you and take this £30. But if you refuse it further, the impression is that, a big Chief like you wants to make money with his duaghter. This will badly let you down and earn you the name "MONEY MONGER"

CHIEF COOKEY: Misisi this no be like your words. You talk true now. Me I bi richman, I no want people to talking that I no rich, na yim make I want to making money with my daughter. I no go

30

take up to £30 from Ototofioko. Make he
bring £20 only. People dey tell me bad
thing about Otofioko na yim make me
callam thief thief. Otofioko forgive me. I
go help you in life. Me be richman big
Chief. Bring the £20.

OTOTOFIOKO: (*smiling*) Chief have the twenty pounds.
(he give the twenty pounds and Chief
Cookey accepts it.)

CHIEF COOKEY: Ototofioko you can go now with my
daughter. She don be your wife. No palaver
again. Live in peace with her.

CECILIA: I am happy now that things have been
peacefully settled. God is wonderful. May
glory be to him. Mr. Ototofioko, you will
be going now with your wife, my daughter
and leaving me with no doubt that you will
live to my expectations.

It is my hope that you will live with
happiness, peace and prosperity with my
daughter. May God bless this marriage for
Christ sake.
Cookey, Elizabeth, Ototofioko: *Amen*.

(EXIT ELIZABETH AND OTOTOFIOKO)

CURTAIN FALLS.

SCENE VII
IN OTOTOFIOKO'S HOUSE

OTOTOFIOKO: My dear, I am happy that our marriage has been peacefully done. Our minds are settled. God has anwered our prayers. His will has been done.

The day that God created man.

He was made to live with a woman

In love and in peace

As husband and wife.

Two heads are better than single.

Every man should marry a wife

To do as his father has done.

Marriage should start with true love

As to make it successful.

A good wife honour her husband

And make life more abundant.

An ideal wife is a wefe who can

share the sorrows of her husband with him;

A wife who is sympahtetic and helpful.

32

My dear no doubt you are one of the best ideal wife.

ELIZABETH: My hus., you are wise. All you said are correct. I have said that you are an orator and very clever. You have no eqaul, unbeatable.
We must give thanks to God for, He has answered our Prayers.
One with him is majority
Now we are recognised husband and wife.
I am now the happiest person on earth.
Who is happier than me? No body.

My dear whenevere I offend you, please for the sake of our deep love, tell me, I must apologise. I hate anything that can offend you, and I will never like to hurt your feelings. It is my hope not to go against your instructions to me. I promise to please you with all the services at my disposal.

My mother told me several time that friendship is easier to make than marriage. In the case of marriage, she said, there are some problems in it. But I firmly believe that we should never quarrel seriously. If atall we would ever have any minor misunderstanding, we should not allow anybody to know. My dear

33

let's make this our marriage the first of its
kind. Let's teach other people that time
has gone when husband and wife quarrel
and fight every now and then.

OTOTOFIOKO: My dear, I thank God to have given
me such an ideal wife like you. It is indeed
a blessing and a "win of raffle." Your
qualities are enviable ones I am very very
happy. May glory be to God. He has
answered me my prayer. Next Sunday I
will denote five guineas in the Church. My
dear, it is true that friendship is easier to
make than marriage. There are certain times
that husband and wife misunderstand
themselves. As a result quarrel starts. In
most cases, the cause of such quarrel is
lack of love among the couples. We love
ourselves and we cannot suffer misunder-
standings. We will enjoy the marriage. It
will be successful and enviable.

My dear, I will never disapoint you and
I hope that you will never disappoint me.
I promise to treat you with love, kindness
and sympathy. I will respect you and your
own rights. I will make you happy. I will
like whatever you like and dislike whatever
you dislike.

34

My dear, please whenever you need to buy anything tell me. Make your needs known to me at any time. I must never forget the £6 you gave to me. Only very few lovers can do that.

My dear, we are now in love competition—-as to whom can love the other greater. I will be trying to show you more love. Well my sweetheart and wife, if you want to compete with me, well let's see what the situation may look like.

My dear nothing can separate us. Some people say that death separates two people. In this our own case, death can't do it. After our life times we shall continue to love ourselves, eighter in Heaven or where the deads stay. If God declares me righteous on the Judgment day, I will never be happy in the Paradise or in the Heaven without you. If I am to stay in Hell, my sorrows or physical sufferings will become more painful or serieus without seeing you. I can laugh at the face of any difficulty or agony as far as I glance at you. You have already stolen my heart. I think of you at any second.

My dear, I don't eat regularly these days, yet become well refreshed. This is the evidence of happiness. Anybody who is

always happy may not be eating too much
but he will be strong, healthy and refreshed.
I am always very happy this time because
of love. The more I look at you, the more
I am happy, strong and refreshed. Thank
you my ideal wife for all you have been
doing to please me and make me swim
in the golden river of happiness.

My sweetheart and dear wife, let us now
join our lips and go to bed. (They kiss
crossing their hands behind each other)

CURTAIN FALLS

SCENE VIII
IN A HOTEL

(After six months of the happy marriage,
Ototofioko and Elizabeth's love becomes
more wonderful "than ever." A friend of
Mr. Ototofioko, Mr. Dick Belgan, throws a
special cocktail party in Rendezvous Hotel
in order to mark the marriage. Relatives,
friends and well wishers are invited. The
guest of honour—*Mr. and Mrs Ototofioko
arrive in English dress.* Every thing well
arranged in the Hotel. (All seats fill to capa-
city by invitees.)

36

FUNCTION OPENS

MASTER OF CEREMONY: I am the master of ceremony and before saying any other words of interest, I wish to introduce the Chairman of this function. (He introduces the chairman who stands up) He is Mr. Felix Anwuna, the chairman of the Development Co-operation. Chairmanship is in this blood. Other guests laught and clap hands for the gentle man.) M. C. sits down.

CHAIRMAN: Ladies and gentlemen. Good evening everybody. Welcome. You have nothing to regret in your coming here this evening instead you get the highest joy.

Ladies and gentlemen, it is within my pleasure to introduce before you the guests of honour. Many of us don't know them I believe. (He introduces Mr. and Mrs Oto-tofioko. Hands claped and long cheers.)

Ladies and gentlemen everybody is happy this evening. Let me introduce to you Mr. Dick Belgan who throws this special cook-tail party. (*He stands Mr. Belgan up.*) This is the gentleman. He is a bossom friend of Mr. and Mrs Ototofioko. He is a Sub-Inspec-tor of Police. He is sociable and a kind man (*cheers.*) Mr. Belgan sits down.

37

Ladies and gentlemen, I am not here to say the inner side of the life story of Mr. and Mrs. Ototofioko, but I will tell you that Mr. and Mrs. Ototofioko love themselves. They can't do without each other, They act like twins. To them, marriage is a simple and happy thing, they have no worries. The marriage of Mr. and Mrs. Ototofioko is enviable and any other couple that copy their example will succeed in marriage.

Ladies and gentlemen, before saying any other thing, we would first hear the voice of Mr. Ototofioko. Attendants can begin to serve beer and cigarettes

ATTENDANTS START TO SERVE

OTOTOFIOKO: Ladies and gentlemen, I do not know how best to express my happiness this evening. My wife and I welcome all of you and cordially thank you very much for you attendance of this occassion.

The honourable chairman has said many things of interest about me and my wife. I do not know that I and my wife have been able to impress the public by the way we live as husband and wife.

Ladies and gentlemen, please join me and my dear wife to thank Mr. Dick Belgan who throws this cocktail party in order to mark my marriage. I am greatful and the love which he has shown me and my wife would long remain in our memories.

I have nothing to say this evening with regards to my lovely marriage with my wife. I pray that we may continue to live in peace and happiness and I wish all of you to live in peace, happiness and prosperity with your wives. No gain in quarrels than loss.

Guest clap hands for him with cheers.

BELGAN: Ladies and gentlemen, I have nothing to say just to add little to what the speakers have said. My friend Mr. Ototofioko married his wife after some struggle, because nothing good without labour.

I am happy that those I invited to this function attended. I am greatful. I have just arranged this small function in order to mark the marriage of my friend, Mr. Ototofioko of the Ministery of Communications and Aviation. I hope that Mr. and Mrs. Ototofioko would continue to love themselves forever. May God bring love, peace, good health and long life in all homes for Christ sake.................

39

GUESTS: Amen, (*they clap hands:*)

CHAIRMAN: Ladies and gentlemen, this is inevitably dance time. Get ready with your wives and dear ones to dance beautiful "highlife" records. Hotel Manager put music, (the Manager puts record and everybody begin to dance.) The dance lasts for 30 minutes and everybody goes, saying Good-bye to each other.

CURTAIN FALLS

The End.

Thanks For Reading

BOOKS PUBLISHED

BY

A. ONWUDIWE & SONS

Love is Infalliable	3s 6d	Nett
Tshombe of Katanga	3s 6d	,,
Too late Cousin	3s 6d	,,
The Labour of Man	1s 6d	,,
Boys and Girls of Nowadays	2s 6d	,,
Marbel the Sweet Honey that Drops Away	3s 6d	,,
To Rule is A Trouble	2s 0d	,,
Agnes in the Game of True Love	2s 0d	,,
Miss Rosy in the Romance of True Love	2s 6d	,,
Family Birth Register	1s 6d	,,
Dr. Zik in the Battle for Freedom	3s 6d	,,
The Disappointed Lover	2s 6d	,,
The Last Days of Lumumba	3s 6d	,,
The Sorrows of Love	2s 6d	,,
How to Write Love Letters	3s 6d	,,
Elizabeth my Lover	2s 6d	,,

Others in Preparations

WHAT WOMEN
ARE THINKING
ABOUT MEN

NO. 1 BOMB TO WOMEN

Net Price 5/-

WHAT WOMEN
ARE THINKING
ABOUT MEN

NO. 1 BOMB TO WOMEN

By

J. O. Nnadozie.

EDITOR.   *OKENWA OLISAH*

Copies Obtainable from:

J. C. BROTHERS BOOKSHOP
26, New Market Road,
ONITSHA/NIGERIA

Net Price: 5s

Contents

Introduction

All lovers of truth, and impartial observer would agree with me that our women do not play "LOVE" in its natural way.

They love to kick boys like football. All they think always is how to trick a man. They have been succeeding, because some men have not know how trickish women are.

Good women are some of the speakers in this pamphlet. When you read them, you will learn that they are annoyed over what their fellow women are doing towards their husbands and to the men in general.

Women can't tell you the truth, but if you master them, they can't deceive you. This is my first work and I promise to produce more works of this nature.

J. O. NNADOZIE

FORWARD

JEO CONGRATS!

May you allow me to say that this little but effective pamphlet is wonderful. The author, Mr. Joseph O. Nnadozie is creative writer and deserves congratulation. If Mr. Joe Nnadozie is not yet eligible to be called a scientist or a pysiologist, he shall in no distant time be qualified.

OKENWA OLISAH

The Editor

WHAT WOMEN ARE THINKING ABOUT MEN

SAID BY ROSE MARY, THE SPEAKER AND SECRETARY GENERAL OF WOMEN.

Rose speaks while Comfort looks on

I am always worried in mind whenever I hear from men that women are the cause of a man's poverty and that a man who don't die because of women will live long life.

I am not at all happy to hear this from men.

Women are not at all created to be the enemies of men. We are created to help men, to be under them and to obey them. We are always thinking about the progress and happiness of men. May God give all men long life and money in order to think very fair of women.

Let the poor men be rich tomorrow and get money to marry women who have not got husbands. There are so many unmarried women nowadays. Women are many but men are few.

By Rose-Mary.

No. 1 BOMB TO WOMEN BY MR. EMMANUEL EZE. THE WOMEN CHALLENGER.

Women are liars and great deceivers. They are not steady. They are not trust-worthy people. They cannot keep secrets. They are the cause of some men's poverty. They are great pretenders, when they tell you yes they mean no.

Their ways are not straight. Many men have been deceived and disappointed by some women. Those men who used them as pillows are sleeping on hard stones. Their ways are wonderful. They have no respect for anybody, even some of those who are married don't respect their husbands.

Some of them are money mongers. They do not love men but their money. They like money as monkey likes banana. Men do suffer and know how to work hard for money but woman know how to eat and buy sweet things with money.

When you marry a new woman she will be calling you master but when she stays long with you, she calls you the father of Rose or John.

Please men, know yourselves for some women are very dangerous. If you are not careful you become useless. Things of nowadays are very hard.

MY WORDS TO MEN ABOUT WOMEN

Men, know yourselves for things are hard. No man can say that he does not like the affairs of women and no woman can say that she does not like the affairs of men. As gold is to John so it is to Rose.

A person who plays with a hungry lion must know that his death is near. Beware of women but don't hate them. Love them, play with them but know when they come to deceive you. Those who communicate with women must spend too much.

Beware of public woman for they are the traps from where your enemy gets you. A woman cannot love you if you don't spend for her. If you get money, you get beautiful women.

No money, no woman. A man who likes to receive women visitors likes to spend. A woman should want you to dash her something even though when she is richer than you. A person who carelessly lost his golden ring in the river must never blame the river but himself.

WOMEN'S CONFERENCE ON MEN

ROSE MARY: I wonder why I find it quite
difficult to trust men. They can say many things
and mean only a few. They mock at women
who do them some good.

9

They seem to be finding harsh treatments against women. I do not like to be wicked to any man. But any man who wants that, I will surely give it to him. My fellow women, I cannot tell what we shall do with particularly the rough set of people.

COMFORT: I know how best to handle them. Last time, I staged war with two rough young men who I can assure you were indeed unfortunate. They tought me to be in the group of the gentle ladies who would like to tolerate foolish talk.

Really, I am well convinced, that as the statures and faces of people vary, so too opinions and character differ. I was very kind to some men at first.

I used to buy clothes for some of my male friends and spend for them at such rate, that only a sister can do so for a brother. My rewards afterwards was nothing but fighting, quarrelling and damnation. One of them whom I very much loved, told me one day that he don't love me again. *He continued:*

Do not come to my house again, bloody fool! I thought that he might have had some defect in the brain. At any rate, I came to discover that, he was quite normal. Earlier, he had promised me marriage.

Everything was later on shattered. He at once went and paid the bride price on one lady and had her wedded. That was my first blow. The ungreatful man ordered me to return his pictures to him.

Further, he wrote thus – "My dear Angela, At first, I had a very high opinion of you and thought that it would be something reasonable to keep with you for some time until I get married. Perhaps, you were happy when I told you that I would marry you.

That of course, was one of the best ways I considered fit to use in deceiving women. Fot if I did not do so or flatter you, it could not have been possible for me to get all the benefits that I have deserved from you. I am now sure of myself and so will no longer want you. I do not want to see you in my house again and my wife will not be happy to see you too. Good bye now. I say to useless life. Welcome to a complete change for good. I do not want your monkey love any more. Return my pictures. Let no memory of my person linger in your mind.

If you allow it to, then it simply means that you are wasting your own time. That of course will not pay you. It is at the same time a way of getting yourself punished. I hope that you will understand this letter well and act accordingly.

Yours formerly in love, Benett." Such a letter is even worse than cutting of my neck at once. For, I love Benett dearly and it is quite strange and shocking to see him behave in this way.

I had been advised by one other lady, to approach some native doctors and apply a charm on him so that he can become a useless man in the life. Another woman suggested to me, that it would be good to steal into his room when he is asleep, arrange with his servant and use a dagger on him.

12

But I am a christian and so, would not like to shed blood. Any way, either of the two methods is good, since he did me wrong first and perhaps had planned to render me useless. I therefore advice my fellow women to be very careful for men are dangerous.

VIOLET: Please, talk no more my dear. I have recently deserted my husband. He is one man who calls himself a business man. Eh! I have seen something. Somebody who talks of business no clothes, no chairs, no food and nothing indeed, tangible.

Well, I have seen businessmen. His own must have been a very different kind altogether. One day, I told him to bring money for soup making. He simply replied that there was no money available and that I should go and manage up. I looked at him and laughed.

I was not trading and had no sewing machine or even any other source of income, apart from what he would give to me. I remained very hungry. He went out as usual, in the morning and then returned in the night. At once, he asked for food. I frankly told him that there was none. He became offended and rushed out to one hotel and ate to his satisfaction. He also drank up wine to such an extent that I began to wonder if he would not go crazy all through the night.

But it appeared somehow wonderful, that a man who had no money in the house, could return home quite satisfied and tipsy. Well, I began to think that the morning would bring something profitable. I had patiently born the hunger but hope to eat well.

I rather found out something strange. My husband had not even a penny left in his pocket. I was given to understand that he usually went to the hotel, ate and drank on credit basis. It all meant that he could not save up any amount of money at all.

The second day, I also experienced the same thing. I would not like to punish my life or to die of hunger because of getting married to a man. I had to go away. He went along broadcasting falsely that I was the cause of his poverty. Thank God that he did not even tell people that I removed any of his things.

14

He came to my mother and told her that he had been dealing with me in the most satisfactory form. When asked why he thought that I left his house, he simply replied that I might have felt like doing so.

He talked of how he kept on feeding me with a very costly diet everyday. He even said that many a time he kept hungry for the purpose of getting me well satisfied with food. He told my mother that she would profit more and more, if she allowed me to come back to his house in a non-distant period.

My mother revealed to me, all that had been said. I laughed and of course became surprised how a man of such age could go to paint black what is white. While there, he borrowed the sum of two pence from my mother and bought tobacco snuff·

He confessed that he had not eaten since I left his house, as according to him, there was no person to prepare the chop. It was a very wonderful type of thing. A man who had no money to buy even one cup of garri, was given an excuse, a very lame one indeed and something much unconnected with the actual. In fact, it all makes me laugh and I do not know what next to say.

Truly, this is one of the methods that trickish men use to defend themselves. You may now see how some men behave. What I think is that they should not be given the chance to talk of our behaviours in our absence. For many of them are liars who can say anything they like at any time.

For my part, I would not allow any man to have me deceived. I do not want to take them serious, when they talk. One day, I heard two men talking over how they flattered some ladies. The first man said that he cunningly got a costly watch from his lady friend.

Later on, he went to her and told her that it was lost and so hid it right inside his box. The second time, he went to her and got a gold ring, a very costly one, and said that his lady friend was helping him very much and that instead of spending he was being spent for. I began to wonder how well it might be for women to continue doing good. The second man said that he was on the way to play the-same type of game too.

Both of them laughed merrily and said that some men are foolish to be spending for what should be free of charge. They said that those ladies who do not demand money are doing the work of God and commended them highly.

Since it has come to be that those who are kind, are termed foolish. I have determined to be hard hearted and merciless. If it is a sin, then let me be guilty of it.

MARGARET: Well my fellow women, although things are like this at the moment, yet I shall not agree with any of you that might suggest to us that all men behave alike. Some of them might be bad, while others are good. Please suppress

17

your emotions. We are meant to be under men. There is no getting out of it. It is for this sake that I would always appeal for calm and particular discretion while dealing with them. At the same time it ought to be worthy of note, that they are strong while we are weak.

It is not always very possible for us to resist them physically. A man is the pillar of a house. A woman is only there for domestic affairs. A man thinks twice, even when he is so annoyed that he might be tempted to be out for destruction and nothing else than that.

But as you all know, we reason one way. We always look at things and take them to be what they appear to look like. Let us talk about the wickedness of some men, but not to the extent of going to have anything out with them. Remember that some of us are also wicked. That is how they too talk of us. They maintain that we are avaricious. Of course, that seems true enough.

Truly, some of us are so greedy that they will like to eat up all that a man has. That is why men who might has fallen victim to such a wicked act are forced to call us "money mongers"

It is not a thing to be denied or be angry over. It is entirely true. But I assure that the earlier this is stopped, the better our relationships with men becomes good. Personally, I do not think that all men who are talking against some of us, are always on the wrong side.

It is sure that they are doing and saying many things against us with reasons. You know that a person who had been foolish at first, would not like to be so the second time, otherwise he or she will be highly blamed. Some of us here are married while others are not.

It will therefore be a very good thing for those who are married to keep in peace with their respective husbands, and those of us who mainly live out of the pockets of bachelors should respect those people very well.

Respect as I have seen, is something which a reasonable woman should have For true it is, that when the right palm washes the left and vice versa, things at once become square. There are some quick-tempered men, who will not like to tolerate bad actions and so are forceed to act at the slightest provocation.

To me, life seems too short for people to sit down and instead of being in peace, they tend to be in pieces. "Live and let live" is quite a good saying. I am not going to take you far and wide. I shall be prepared to listen to more views if any. But as I have seen that the meeting is rather getting very long, it will be necessary to close up.

But I shall be pleased if we can all put into practice, all we have heard and also discussed today. When trouble gives way to peace and comfort, life becomes more sweet.

(THEY CLOSE UP)

20

It did not take many hours after the meeting, when Rose, "one of those who had attended it came into contact with Jerome. The Lady was fair in complexion, tall and with red lips.

She had never been rough right from her childhood and so was highly spoken of by everywhere in the town. In fact she was a real piece of beauty and no person who saw her, failed to stop in order to look at her beautiful face.

Jerome, had for long, desired to speak to her with the intention of making love with her. The chance had actually come and if he missed it such possibility might not easily come back.

At once he ran into a nearby shop and bought many things including a piece of cloth which cost him up to five pounds and four shillings and gave to her. The lady thanked him, but was surprised why such should be done.

It was then, that the man started to say "My dear lady, for quite a long time now, I have been longing for a way of getting you when alone, so as to have some discussion with you.

Now it appears that the Almighty has sent you. All that I want, is for you to follow me to my house, so that we can discuss matters". "What matters might we go to discuss?", she asked. "Your love and nothing but that" replied Jerome with a low tone and his face full of smiles.

"I am sorry", She said. "I am not that type. It is rather very unfortunate indeed. You may have to try your luck somewhere else. I am just from a meeting where we women discussed in detail what we think of men.

My advice to you is this, if you can only keep yourself quiet and save up some money and marry, you will be one of the happiest men that ever lived. For me to go away with your presents now and later on, turn your request down, might not be a good thing in the sight of God and man.

It is therefore necessary to be frank to you. May you realise that we woman don't force men to spend for us. Rather they go out and put themselves under that expenditure.

Afterwards they begin to regret and we laugh. You should also bear in mind that every person like success. If therefore a person fails, it will be some thing very disgracing.

So please you ought to be very careful how you get along with women. For my part, I would not like to bring ruin to any person except a person who causes himself to run into it. Your piece of cloth can be given back to you.

Your presents can also follow you home. You may be offended at this, but if you think two times, you will agree with me that I am not entirely wrong. These are my own views about men. They say that we talk a great deal. But I can assure you that they talk more. Goodbye.

MRS. ELIZABETH TALKS WHAT WOMEN

THINK

I am a woman but I don't cherish what my fellow women are doing, especially ladies and girls. They think that they are very beautiful, and so make proud before young boys and men. They pretend too much, I know that it is absolutely certain that, it is an inborn of a woman that she cannot first approach a man for either friendship or marriage, no matter how attractive the man may be to her, but this is not a licence for a woman to bluff a man, because he approaches for love.

Our women are not careful in the relationship between man and woman. They are only careful about their dresses. Believe me sincerely, I don't appreciate the tactics and system they apply in making love with men.

In other countries such as England, America, India, France, etc., women of these place are not tough and proud as ours. They won't venture to tell you that they love you if they have animosity on you. They won't tell you that they hate you if they love you. Never life to pretend. In short, they are plain. If they love you, they will tell you straight ahead, and if they hate you, they would tell you straight ahead, no "Panky Nyanky". They never regard love making as a game as my fellow women regard it here in Nigeria. Halt a woman on the street here in Nigeria and tell her: "I want to befriend you," and see her reaction. She may disgrace you because she is not cultured. But in other civilized countries, it is a matter of yes or no.

I know that men have their own faults in love making, but I may say that those faults are negligible ones, not serious as the ones of my fellow women. I believe that men are deeper in love. I quite be aware that many of my fellow women would not like my statements or comment in this pamphlet, but I don't mind, anything can be said against me, truth is always better, and I know that fools do not understand judgement.

These are some words which have helped to spoil and let down women in this country. They say the words to the men in order to disgrace them, but they don't know that they are disgracing themselves. The words are OJUGO, ONA-EKPOYI.

25

These words are offensive, unbecoming, provo-
king, and they are being said to the last at Onitsha.
These words should be abandoned please.

I come to what women are thinking about men.
Women of this country think that men can't do
without them. This is partly wrong though. Men
can't do without women and women can not also
do without men, even men are more important.
It is wrong and primitive to think that women are
not liable to spend for their boy - friends.

I have observed that women of this nation do
not spend anything on or for their boy-friends. It is
scarce to see one of them spend for her boy-friend.
Some poor boys who cannot maintain themselves,
borrow to buy something for their lovers. I criticise
these type of boys here, it is not good to enter debt
inorder to maintain or satisfy a lover.

In other countries where real love intoxicates
women like wine, their women spend for
their lovers without checking; "What has this boy
done to me." They are skilful in the art of
making love but many fellow women here in Nigeria

are not skilful in that, rather they are skilful in the art of bad tactics of making love.

Who are those ladies who call themselves "First class? "First class" on body but not in moral and behaviours. I have to believe that some men who are now marrying two wives each, are not interested in doing so but due to the attitude of their first wives they are forced to do so.

Some of my fellow women here in Nigeria have no good sense. They are trickly obedient and submissive to their husbands when they have not got male child or wed in the Church with their husbands, but authomatically change wonderfully, become rude, sturbborn, disobedient and feel that they have got the house as soon as they deliver a male child or wed in the Church or in the Government. Some attempt to take over the control of their husbands.

It is not only bad for a woman to control her husband but also an abomination. After wedding in the Church or delivering male child some become very confident that their husbands have no mouth to tell them:

27

"Pack and go away" Not knowing that with legal action that it is possible.

My fellow women, it is high time we should realise that our husbands are carrying our burdens and responsibilities. We should do everything possible to delight them. It is not good to displease them in the house. I stop so far. A word is enough for the wise.

Elizabeth K. Igwengo.

A wife to a happy husband.

MRS. JENETH TAKES OVER

Ladies and gentlemen, boys and girls, elders and Natural rulers, citizens and foreigners, I am saluting. I am nobody than Mrs. Jeneth Nwangbo Kedunu. No. 1 challenger of my fellow African women.

I am a woman but I must tell you that I don't like what some are doing. They don't behave well, they behave to the annoyance of men, and even to the annoyance of some few women who are fair. Some women are good but the activities of the bad ones overshadows the realisation that good women exist, women who know

28

the feelings of men, women who respect and honour their husbands. The relation between man and woman is delicate, and so every carefulness must be applied to it, because small thing can spoil it.

I am here calling upon all women to improve in manners and behaviours. I regret that in view of the short space I have in this pamphlet I cannot talk much, and so I end. May God be with you.

— Mrs. Jenett Ifeoma Nwaike.

A loyal wife to a Minister of state.

WHAT MRS. BEATRICE, HEADMISTRESS OF THE NATIONAL GIRLS' SCHOOL AMARAKA, SAYS:

First of all, I like to introduce my-self to you. I am Mrs. Beatrice Okoma, the Headmistress of the National Girls' School, Amaraka, Western Region, Nigeria. I am 29 years old and have taught for 19 years. I am a holder of High Elementary Certificates. I got it 3 years ago. My promise is that I will displine all girls in my School, and contribute much to education in Nigeria.

I have an important advice to give to my fellow women. Before I married, I played love and so I know some in and out of it.

If a man approaches you to befriend you, and you don't like the man either because of his social out-look or that you don't at all want to fall in love with any man, no matter how handsome he may be, use courtesy in declining what the man tells you. Don't use bad words on the man or disgrace him, it is dangerous.

If you disgrace a wicked man he may have no other revenge than to charm on you. If a man whom you like approaches you, you can ask him to give you time to consider or agree, there is no need to waste time. You should ask him his name, occupation and home town. Never ask him his salary.

After getting all these particulars, you tell him what annoys you and what you don't like. Ask him to tell you his, and then proceed with the friendship. Don't fall in love with any other man or boy. Stand one place, run not up and down. Be sincere and faithful to him. At times buy something and send to him.

Don't demand anything from him, take only the thing he gives you out of his mind. Men hate women who demand gifts. In your letters to him be very careful in what you write. Don't say nonsense, immoral words or flatter. Write what is good and presentable to the public in case you have any misunderstanding with the man.

Boys, I am also advising you all to refrain from writing nonsense in your letter to your lovers. You can be judged in the Court with the contents of your letters, if any thing happens between you and your lover. So take time when you write. Don't write in order to please your lover and implicate yourself. The day is dangerous.

—Mrs. Beatrice Okoma.

MR. PETER K. OJUKWU TALKS ABOUT
MARRIAGE PROMISE.

What is promise? Promise is an undertaking to do something. It is bad to promise a girl that you will marry her and after you disappoint her. It is also bad to promise a man that you will marry him and after you disappoint him.

31

Disappointment pains very much. Do you know what is disappointment? It does harm to the dis-appointed. Never disappoint anybody. Before you promise any woman that you will marry her, be sure that you must marry her, don't promise to marry her merely to get her fall in love with you.

This is a deceit and illegal. Remember that when you promise to marry a person, that you have commited yourself, if you fail to do so, you can be sued to Court for damages.

Peter Kebbi Ojukwu, of the Director of

Public Procecution Officer, Ibi.

MR. WILLIAM BELGAM (A EUROPEAN) TALKS ABOUT FRIENDSHIP.

It is easy to make TEN friends a day but it is hard to keep them. What is friend? Friend is one attached to another by effection and esteem; an intimate associate. If the answer is this, why do some people call the people they have only seen for the first sight friends? It is wrong to introduce your client, your customer, your colleague or your mate to somebody, as your friend.
Before you can call some body your friend,

he or she must be your intimate associate. Your life and his agree.

Mr. William Belgam,

President—General, International Friendly Association.

CHIEF DANIEL SAYS, WHAT SPOILS MARRIAGE: GOSSIP IS NO 1

The beginning of marriage sweets like honey. It is called "Honey Moon." But changes of things are got after one year. Sometimes the amount voted for the enjoyment have finished. Perhaps the wife has not yet pregnated. A gossipper is busy suppling his unfounded and false news.

Gossip is No. 1 thing that spoils a family. It spoils marriage, and does a bad work in every thing. So beware of gossippers.

Chief Daniel Ukefika,

Husband of 20 wives.

33

MR. BERNARD NWOKO SAYS THE DANGER
IN MARRYING A VERY YOUNG GIRL:

To marry a very young girl, who have not known good and bad; who have not known likeness, is delicate. She may reject you when she grows up. So marry a girl who has attained the age to know without being told; the age to decide things for herself. — Bernard Nwoko, Affected.

HERE COMES A LETTER FROM PAUL EZE WHO SAID
THAT WOMEN HAVE TAKEN ALL HIS MONEY.
THE LETTER READS:

I am now in a big trouble, I don't know what to do. I have no money to buy my food. Since last two years I have been in love with two beautiful women who call me "THE LONDON BOY". I was not surprised of this big name for my pockets were heavy with

34

money, and I always acted as a rich man inorder to keep my big name "THE LONDON BOY." I always give them money to buy their need. Every Saturday and Sunday I use to hire taxi to take us to many places for sight seeing and we never miss Cinema shows every Saturday.

Now I have lost my job as a teacher from where I got the money. The worst is that I haven't even the sum of 10/- (ten shillings) in my pocket. What shall I do, please advise me.

AUTHOR'S ADVICE:

Thank you very much Mr. Paul Eze. You have acted in a foolish way. So you never heard that no condition is permanent in this world. So you don't know that a government worker must be prepared to leave his office at any time.

When you were a teacher, you spent your money carelessly on beautiful women, who used to call you "THE LONDON BOY" just to enjoy your money. You kept on spending your money when other reasonable men were saving their money. Now poverty must force you to put down your title which the women gave you.

Any way don't loose hope. You can become a labourer or load carrier. But know yourself, the world is hard. If you are not careful, you become useless. A word is enough for the wise.

THE SECOND LETTER COMES FROM ROSE MARY. HER LETTER READ:

Rose Mary,
G. C. T.,
Lagos—Nigeria.

I am in love with a man since last two months The man promised to marry me. Both of us have been sincere to each other. Last two weeks the man borrowed the sum of £10 (ten pounds) from me. Two weeks later, he asked me to give him another sum of £4 (four pounds) and I refused.

He became annoyed with me and told me not to come to his house again. I asked him to give me back the sum of £10 (ten pounds) I gave him, but he refused. He said that he don't know me. What shall I do? Shall I give him another sum of £4 in order to continue our love or shall I put him

36

to court to claim my money. Please advise me.

AUTHOR'S ADVICE:

I am very sorry to notice that the man whom you helped has turned your enemy. The man hasn't true love for you. He promised you marriage just to confuse you. Don't give him the money. I am not going to blame you why you gave him the £10 (ten pouuds).

If you know that the man signed an agreement for the money, you can put him to court and claim your money. But if you know that he did not sign any agreement for it, don't put him to court. You cannot claim it.

What you will do is this, go to him again and ask him to give you the money, if he refuses, call any of your friends to lead you. If he still refuses, put everything in prayer and ask God to do His will. Next time, don't fall in love with men who like to befriend women in order to get money.

THE END

NOTE

Mr. J. O. Nnadozie the original author of this book, has actually to be congratulated for launching out an issue of this nature, which concerns two sections of mankind. As a matter of fact, the affairs relating to man and woman are such that cannot easily be tackled, except through experience and proper study of mankind.

Having been called upon to enlarge the pamphlet I set out to try my best in bringing more points which would help to educate the youths and also assist the grown ups.

FELIX N. STEPHEN

Public Notice

Mr. J. C. Anorue is the only person who has the right to print and sell the copies of this booklet entitled "What Women Are Thinking About Men."

Mr. J. O. Nnadozie "The Author and the former publisher of this booklet has entirely handed it over to Mr. J. C. Anorue.

A Bibliography of
the Pamphlet Literature

List of Abbreviations
B: Biography
Es: Essay
ill: illustrated
Intr: Introduced by
Nar: Narrative
Ro: Romance
Th: Theatre

The publisher and date of publication are included where possible.

Abiakam, J.
How to speak to girls and win their love (Onitsha: J. C. Brothers Bookshop) 48 pp
ill. Es and Th.
*How to write and reply letters for marriage, engagement letters and how to know a
girl to marry* (Onitsha) Es.
Agunanne, A. O.
Love is Immortal.
Ajokuh, Emman Ugochukwu
The Chains of love (Onitsha: Gebo Brothers) 62 pp. Ro.
Albert, Miller O.
Rosemary and the taxi-driver (Onitsha: Chinyelu Printing Press) 43 pp. Nar.
Saturday Night disappointment (Onitsha: Chinyelu Printing Press) 36 pp. Nar.
Anonymous
*The famous treason trial of Awolowo, Enahoro and 23 others together with the
appeal and the last judgment of Awolowo and 16 appelants* (Onitsha: J. C. Brothers
Bookshop) 72 pp. ill. Th.
The Life and work of Dr Zik in Nigeria Republic (Onitsha: J. C. Brothers) 72 pp. ill.
B.
The New Nigerian leader and the biography of African leaders, 54 pp. ill. B.
The Western Nigerian crisis and army take over 1966, 63 pp. Th.
*How to write and reply letters for marriage, engagement letters, love letters, and how
to know a girl to marry* (Onitsha: J. C. Brothers Bookshop) 72 pp. ill. Es.
Anorue, J.
Un-natural death of Chief Manbo.
Anumuda, Leonard O.
Goodbye to British government, Intr: L.N.P. Uzoh (1962) 44 pp. Es. Nar.
Anya, Emman Udegbunam
One love for ever (Onitsha: Tabansi Bookshops, 1959) 62 pp. Ro.
She died in the bloom of youth (Onitsha) 38 pp.
Matter of life and death (Onitsha, 1956) 48 pp. Nar.
Wretched Orphan (1956) 59 pp. Nar.
Anyichie, J. A. Okeke
Adventures of the Four Stars (Onitsha: Highbred Maxwell) 84 pp. Nar.
Aririguzo, Cyril Nwakuna
Miss Appolo's pride leads her to be unmarried – 'Pride goeth before a fall'.
Miss Comfort's heart cries for Tony's love (Onitsha) 23 pp.
Steps for the freedom of Nigeria (Onitsha) 12 pp. Th.
The work of love (Onitsha: Aririguzo & Sons) 53 pp. Th.
Aroye, Momoh
Awolowo and Akintola in political crisis.

Concise biography of His Excellency the Governor-General and Commander-In-Chief of the Federation of Nigeria. B.
Nancy in blooming beauty. Ro.

Aroye, Momoh and Aliche, D. Wac
The lady who robbed her mother to defend her husband (Onitsha: Atlantic Printers) 30 pp. ill. Nar.

Asika, D. O.
Public Road.

Azike, B. S.
False promise in marriage and its punishment. 'You must marry me' demanded Miss Rose (Onitsha: B. U. Okereke s.a.) 43 pp. Nar.

Azoh, D. A.
A colourful wedding and a happy home.

Azubuike, Eusebuis A.
How to make meetings.

Bubagha, Stephen Owen MacDonald
The roaming sisters: a story of three school girls who for ambition desired hotel-life and two of whom eventually ended in tears and sorrows (Aba: Aut., 1958) 36 pp.
Bad men and bad women.
Pocket encyclopaedia of etiquette and commonsense.

Chiazor, Benjamin O.
Back to happiness (Onitsha: Highbred Maxwell) 52 pp. Ro.
How to be the friend of girls (Onitsha: Highbred Maxwell) 52 pp. Ro.

Chidia, (Challinbur) G. P.
Her evening tales.
Marry with love.
Queen of night; a very romantic novel (Port Harcourt, 1957) Ro.
We three sisters (Port Harcourt: Aut., 1957).

Chinaka, B. A.
The life of Dr Nkrumah, Dr Chike Obi and other leaders in Nigeria (Onitsha: Njoku and Sons Bookshop) 48 pp. ill. B.
How to speak and write to girls for friendship (Onitsha).

Ebere, P. P.
Suffers of Africans: a complete history of white imperialism towards Africans nationalism (Onitsha: Agbai & Sons) 33 pp. Es and Th.

Egemonye, Joseph N. C.
Broken Engagement (Onitsha, 1959) Nar.
Disaster in the realms of love (Onitsha: Tabansi Bookshop, 1958).

Ekesiobi, Eddy N.
True love. Fineboy Joe and beautiful Kathe, Intr.: Okeanu and William Oshogwe (Port Harcourt: V. C. Okeanu, 1954) 57 pp. Nar.

Ekwensi, C. O. D.
Ikolo the wrestler and other Ibo tales (Onitsha) Nar.
When love whispers, Intr.: Funmilayo Ransome-Kuti (Onitsha: Tabansi Bookshop) 44 pp. Nar.

Eze, Charles N.
Little John in the love adventure (Onitsha: Lawrence N. I. Igwebuike) 40 pp. Nar.

Eze, K. C.
Why modern boys and girls are careless, Intr.: Obiaga (Onitsha: A. Onwudiwe & Sons) 72 pp., ill. Ro.
How to write love letters and win girls' love for friendship.
Our interesting Ibo native laws and customs.
The way and how to conduct meetings (Onitsha: Gebo & Brothers) 56 pp. Es.

Ezimora, Justin
The lady that forced me to be romantic (Onitsha) Ro.

Ibekwe, Daniel O.
Justice in Chunderland (Yaba: Aut.) 28 pp. ill. Th.

Ibekwe, G. Azubuike
Man know thyself (Onitsha) Es.

Ibekwe, I. M. U.
How to conduct meetings (Onitsha: Igu).
Iguh, Thomas Orlando
The disappointed lover (Onitsha: A. Onwudiwe & Sons) 60 pp. ill. Th.
Love at first, hate at last (Onitsha: Gebo Brothers) 49 pp. Th.
£9,000,000,000 man still says no money (Onitsha: Highbred Maxwell) 52 pp. Th.
The prize of love (Onitsha: Njoku and Sons Bookshop) 28 pp. Th.
The sorrows, complete treason and last appeal of Chief Awolowo and others (Onitsha: Aut.) 68 pp. Th.
The sorrows of love (Onitsha: A. Onwudiwe and Sons) 40 pp. Nar.
The struggles and trials of Jomo Kenyatta (Onitsha: Appolos and Bros.) 56 pp. Th.
Tshombe of Katanga, Intr.: Matthew A. Umejili (Onitsha: Onwudiwe & Sons) 54 pp. ill. Th.
Agnes in the game of true love (Onitsha) 35 pp.
Alice in the romance of love (Onitsha).
Why men never trust women.
Dr Zik in the battle for freedom.
John in the romance of true love. A tragical drama from West Africa for Schools and colleges (Onitsha) 48 pp.
The last days of Lumumba (Onitsha, 1961) 59 pp.
Agnes the faithful lover.
Dr Nkrumah in the struggle for freedom (Onitsha: Highbred Maxwell) 68 pp. Th.
Ike, Akwaelimo
Great men of Iboland (Aba: Aut., 1952) 38 pp. B.
Ikeagu
Memoirs of Israel Njemanze.
Ikpoto, G.
Chukwuma in the habit of chasing.
Kamalu, Sigis
The surprise packet (Port Harcourt: V. C. Okeanu) 60 pp. Ro.
Kpalaku, C. W.
Beautiful Adanma in crazy love.
Madu, N. O.
Miss Rosy in the romance of true love (Onitsha: A. Onwudiwe & Sons) 31 pp. Nar.
Maduekwe, Joseph C.
Ngozi brings new life to her parents (Aba, 1962) 28 pp.
Madumere, Adiele
Love is infallible (Port Harcourt: Aut., 1955) 72 pp. Ro.
The way to make friends with girls (Onitsha: A. Onwudiwe & Sons) 32 pp. Nar.
Maxwell, Highbred
Forget me not, Intr.: Thomas A. Obi. (Onitsha: Aut.) 56 pp. Nar.
The gentle giant 'Alakuku' (Onitsha: Students Own Bookshop) 26 pp. Nar.
Our modern ladies' characters towards boys: the most exciting novel with love letters, drama, telegram and campaigns of Miss Beauty to the teacher asking him to marry her (Onitsha: Students' Own Bookshop, 1959) 23 pp.
Public opinion on lovers (Onitsha: 1962) 46 pp. Nar.
Wonders shall never end (Onitsha: 1962) 32 pp. ill.
Back to happiness (Onitsha).
Guides for engagement (Onitsha: Aut.) 27 pp. Es. and Th.
Money Palaver (Onitsha: Aut).
Mba, A. N.
The life story of Zik (Onitsha: Appolos Brothers, 1961) 32 pp. B.
The treasonable felony trial of Chief Awolowo and twenty others (Onitsha: Appolos Brothers, 1963) 40 pp. ill. Th.
The famous story and murder of John Kennedy, Intr.: A. B. C. Ononiwu (Onitsha: Appolos Brothers Press) 46 pp. ill. B. and Nar.
Nduka, T. I.
Julius Nyerere: A profile (Aba: Goodhope Printing Press) 26 pp. B.
Ngbanti, Jackson B.
So great is my tragedy (s.1: Aut.) 55 pp. ill. B and A.

Ngoh, John E. A.
Florence in the river of temptation, Intr.: L. U. Ukwu, John E. A. Ngoh and E. F. Briggs (Onitsha: Century printing press, 1960) 40 pp.
Njoku, Nathan
A guide to marriage.
Beware of women.
How to succeed in life.
How to write better letters, applications and business letters.
How to write good English letters and compositions.
How to write letters. 'Love is a warm affection'.
How to write love letters.
My seven daughters are after young boys. A classical drama for schools and colleges (Onitsha: Njoku and Sons s.a.) 40 pp. ill.
Why boys don't trust their girl friends.
Nkwocha, Sylvester Kingsley
Young rascal (Aba) 36 pp.
Nnadozie, J. O.
Beware of harlots and many friends. The world is hard (Onitsha) 43 pp. ill. Es and Nar.
What women are thinking about men. No. 1 bomb to women, Intr.: Okenwa Olisah (Onitsha: J. O. Nnadozie) 15 pp.
Nnani, Francis and Christopher E.
Never lose hope (Onitsha: Varsity Bookshop), 13 pp. Nar.
Should we love the painted sepulchre? (Onitsha: Varsity Publishing Co.) 54 pp. ill. Ro.
Nnama, Bedford C. C.
Freedom.
Still alive yet buried.
Nwala, G. H. A. Obi
Susanne 'The one in town' Part I.
The iniquity and trial of Awolowo.
Nwankwo, Gilbert
Tragic love and the woman from nowhere (Yaba: Aut.) 48 pp. Nar.
Nwankwo, Mazi Raphael D. A.
The bitterness of politics and Awolowo's last appeal (Onitsha: A. Onwudiwe & Sons) 106 pp. ill. B.
Nwigwe, Henry Emezuem
Corner corner love: Ajayi and Janet. A prized fiction booklet (Yaba) 40 pp.
Nwosu, Cletus Gibson
Miss Cordelia in the romance of destiny. The most sensational love destiny that has ever happened in West Africa. (Enugu: Aut, 1958) 40 pp.
Nzeako, J. U. Tagbo
Rose darling in the garden of love, Intr.: Sunny Okolo and Tommy A. Asiegbu (Onitsha: Tabansi Bookshop, 1961) 29 pp. Nar.
Obiaga, C. C.
Boys and girls of nowadays (Onitsha: A. Onwudiwe & Sons) 43 pp. ill. Nar.
Obikwelu, G. N.
Pendant smiles (Enugu, 1959) 29 pp.
Continuation of pendant smiles (Umuahia, 1960) 46 pp.
Obioha, R. I. M.
Beauty is a trouble (Onitsha).
Between love and obedience (Onitsha: Gebo and Brothers).
Friendship between boys and girls (Onitsha.)
Friendship between boys and girls and how to make it.
Man must work.
Money hard to get because the world is hard.
Sylvanus Olympio (the assassinated President of Togo Republic) (Onitsha, 1964) 54 pp. Th.
Obiyo, Anthony Kemno
June for all Junes (Owerri, 1952) 7 pp.

Odili, Edmund
Mystery of the missing sandals (1953) 24 pp. ill.
Odili, F. E.
What is life? – (What each survivor is subject to ask selfly –) (Onitsha) 64 pp. Es. and Nar.
Odioh, N.
Edith in the flower of love, Intr.: Sigis Kamalu and V. C. Okeanu (Port Harcourt: V. C. Okeanu) 31 pp. Th.
Odoemele, Onyekwere
Love without conscience: a heart-rending love story (Kafanchan, 1951) 75 pp.
Ogali, O. A.
Agnes the faithful lover.
Eddy the coal-city boy (Uzuakoli, 1959) 27 pp.
Okeke the magician (Uzuakoli, 1958) 39 pp.
Patrice Lumumba (Enugu, 1961) 32 pp. Th.
Mr. Rabbit is dead (Ovim, 1958) 40 pp.
Caroline the One guinea girl (Enugu, 1960) 33 pp. ill. Nar.
The life history of Alhaji Adegoke Adelabu (Uzuakoli, 1958) 33 pp.
Veronica my daughter (Enugu, 1956) 40 pp.
Long long ago (Ovim, 1957) 20 pp.
Smile awhile (Enugu, 1957) 20 pp.
No heaven for the priest (Enugu, 1970) 36 pp. Es.
The Ghost of Patrice Lumumba (Enugu, 1961) 42 pp. ill. Th.
Angelina my darling. Th.
Adventures of Miranda. Nar.
The voice of love. Nar.
Igwe the politician. Th.
Do you know them? Gen. Know.
The road to success. Es.
Ihi na ofo na ogu nke ndi igbo.
The love that fights. Th.
Adventures of Constable Joe. Th.
Adanma Nwam (Ibo Play). Th.
Is this politics? Es.
Ogu, H. O.
The love that asks no questions (Warri, 1958) 23 pp.
Return of Evelyn in a drama on how I was about marrying my sister (Aba, 1960) 42 pp.
Rose only loved my money (Aba, 1960) 32pp.
Why Okafor sacked his wife (Aba, 1960) 42 pp.
Jonny the most worried husband (Aba: Treasure press) 26 pp. Nar.
Okeke and his master's girl-friend (Aba: G. C. Moneme, 1960) 38 pp. Th.
How a passenger collector posed and got a lady teacher in love (Aba: G. C. Moneme, 1961) 36 pp. Nar.
Why some rich men have no trust in some girls (Aba: G. C. Moneme) 43 pp. Nar.
Why women have no trust in men (Aba: Confidence printing press and Balance Bookshop) Nar.
Oguanobi, Ralph
Two friends in the romance of runaway lover (Onitsha: Martin Asiemeonwu) 25 pp. ill. Nar.
Ohaejesi, M. Chidi
How to write love letters and win girls' love (95 love letters and how to compose them).
Ohaejesi, M. N.
The sweetness and kingdom of love.
Oji, B. A.
Africanism, the fundamental of African religion.
From fear to confidence.
General methods of teaching and class management.
Ibo girls.

Originality of religion revealed.
Passport to a happy life.
Social and political history of Nigeria.
Testimonies of reincarnation.
The age of bribery.
The government of the headmaster for practical school organisation.

Okeanu, Vincent C.
Nancy in blooming beauty, Intr.: V. C. Okeanu and the Penman's Editorial and Novel Syndicate (Port Harcourt, 1961) 38 pp. ill. Nar.

Okeke, Alex. Obiorah
I'll rather break my sword and die (Onitsha: Highbred Maxwell) 72 pp. ill. Th.

Okeke, E. N.
Sorrow for student.

Okenwa Olisa
Many Things You Must Know About Ogbuefi Azikiwe and Republican Nigeria (Onitsha, 1964).

Okenwa, M.
Boy's life of Zik: the President of Nigeria Republic (Onitsha: Gebo & Brothers) 36 pp. B.

Okonkwo, Rufus
About boys and girls, Intr.: Emmanuel Adibenma & R. Okonkwo (Onitsha: J. C. Brothers) 39 pp. Nar.
The game of love: a classical drama from West Africa, Intr. J. O. Nnadozie (Onitsha: J. C. Brothers) 49 pp. Nar.
How to make friends with girls (Onitsha: J. C. Brothers) 48 pp. ill. Th.
Man works hard for money, Intr.: J. C. Anoruo (Onitsha: J. C. Anoruo) 40 pp. Es. and Nar.
Never trust all that love you (Onitsha, 1961) 44 pp.
Why boys never trust money-monger girls, Intr.: Emmanuel Adibenma (Onitsha: J. C. Brothers Bookshop) 39 pp. Es. and Nar.
The way to avoid poverty (Onitsha) Es. and Nar.

Okonyia, Chike
Tragic Niger Tales.

Okoye, Daniel I. Tonny
Alice the perfect romancer (Aba: Ofomata's printing press, 1962) 56 pp.

Olisa (Olisah), Sunday) Okenwa (Pseud. 'Strong Man of the Pen')
About the husband and wife who hate themselves (Onitsha: Aut. sole agent) 51 pp; also (Onitsha: Highbred Maxwell sole agent) 50 pp. Th.
Drunkards believe bar is heaven (Onitsha: Chinyelu printing press) 16 pp. Es. and Nar.
Dangerous man, Vagabond versus Princess (Onitsha: Aut., 1960) 16 pp. ill.
Elizabeth my lover (Onitsha: A. Onwudiwe & Sons) 40 pp. Th.
The half-educated court messenger (Onitsha: Nathan Njoku, 1960) 20 pp.
How Lumumba suffered in life and died in Katanga (Onitsha: P. E. Unaigwe) 53 pp. ill B. Nar.
How to know who loves you and hates you. Man is an untrustworthy being. (Onitsha: Nigerian Commercial Service) 20 pp. Es. Nar.
How to live better life and help yourself (Onitsha: Okenwa Publications) 40 pp. Nar. Th. Es.
Love your brother and remember the last day (Blood is too costly, great and power), by the Strong Man of the Pen (Onitsha: Prince E. Madumelu) 40 pp. ill Es. and Nar.
The life in the prison yard: 'It is a hard life'. The prisoner Mr Okorinta who escaped from the White College tells the story (Onitsha: Aut.) 19 pp. Nar.
The life story and death of Mr Lumumba (Onitsha: B. C. Okara & Sons Bookshop) 55 pp. ill. B.
Man has no rest in his life. Since the world is broken into pieces, truth is not said again (Onitsha: B. C. Okara & Sons) 38 pp. Es.
Money palaver, by Master of Life (Money Master) (Onitsha: Highbred Maxwell) 22 pp. Es. and Nar.

No condition is perfect, by the Master of Life. Money maketh a man, a dress maketh a woman (Onitsha, 1957) 10 pp.
Story about mammy-water (Onitsha, 1960) 17 pp.
Trust no-body in time because human being is trickish. Human being is deep, difficult to know and full of disappointments. (Onitsha: Prince Madumelu) 52 pp. ill. Es. and Nars.
The world is hard, by the Master of Life (Onitsha, 1957) 24 pp.
How to live bachelor's life and girl's life without much mistakes (Onitsha).
Life turns man up and down – money and girls turn man up and down (Onitsha).
Man suffers (Onitsha).
Money hard but some women don't know (Onitsha, 1963).
Money hard to get but easy to spend (Onitsha, 1964).
N.C.N.C. and N.P.C. in political war over 1963 census figures (Onitsha).
The Ibo native law and custom (Onitsha).
The life history of Anglican Youth Fellowship (Onitsha).
The way to get money.
Oloyede, S. P.
The trial of Hitler (Aba: International press) 12 pp. Th.
Omoruyi, P.
My life in the bush.
Omuamu, Sampson A.
From the cradle to the grave (Enugu, 1959) 24 pp.
Ononuju, Michael C.
Purest of the pures (Aba: Ofomata's press, 1960) 48 pp.
Onuoha, C. N. (pseud. C. N. O. Money-Hard)
Why harlots hate married men and love bachelors (Port Harcourt: Aut.) 32 pp. ill. Es.
Onwudiegwu, J. K.
The bitterness of love.
Onwudiwe, A (pseud. 'Speedy Eric', 'Young Dynamic Author')
The art of love in real sense, Intr.: Victor and Grace (Onitsha: A. Onwudiwe & Sons) 61 pp. Ro.
Mabel the sweet honey that poured away (Onitsha: A. Onwudiwe & Sons) 72 pp. ill. Ro.
The history of the African leaders. Biography, 54 pp. ill. B.
Onwuka, Wilfred
The famous treason trial of Awolowo, Enahoro and 23 others (Onitsha: J. C. Brothers) 52 pp. ill. B.
The famous treason trial of Awolowo.
The life story and death of John Kennedy, Intr.: Martin I. Okoroji (Onitsha: J. C. Brothers) 52 pp. ill. B.
The life history and last journey of President John Kennedy (Onitsha: Gebo & Brothers) 60 pp. B.
Orizu, Okwudili (pseud. Ayo Mac Donald)
The joy of life and its merriments (Onitsha: Highbred Maxwell) 37 pp. Th.
The labour of man.
The mirror of life (Onitsha: J. C. Anorue & Sons) 24 pp. Nar.
To rule is a trouble.
Oti, Penn C. I.
£75,000 and 7 years imprisonment (Onitsha: B. A. Ezuma) 20 pp. Nar.
Richards, A.
How to marry a good girl and live in peace with her.
Raphael, Raja
How to start life and end it well (Onitsha: Gebo & Brothers) 47 pp. Es. and Th.
The right way to approach ladies and get them in love (Onitsha: Appolos Brothers) 52 pp. Es.
Trial of Awolowo and 23 others together with his appeal (Onitsha: Gebo & Brothers) 56 pp. B. and Nar.
Stephen, Felix N.
A fool at forty (Port Harcourt: Vincent Okeanu) 42 pp. Nar.

A journey into love (Onitsha: Chinyelu printing press) 52 pp. Ro.
A woman's pride is her husband.
Be careful! salutation is not love. 'Never trust all now-a-days' (Onitsha: Njoku & Sons) 40 pp. Es. and Nar.
Beautiful Maria in the act of true love. 'Emma and Maria' (Onitsha: Michael Allan Ohaejesi) 40 pp. Th.
Experience in life is key to success.
How to avoid enemies and bad company.
How to get a lady in love (Onitsha: Njoku & Sons Bookshop) 57 pp. ill. Th.
How to get a lady in love and romance with her (Onitsha).
How to play love (Onitsha: Njoku & Sons) 56 pp. Ro.
How Tshombe and Mobutu regretted after the death of Mr. Lumumba.
Lack of money is not lack of sense.
The African Youth's Guide.
The life and story of boys and girls (Onitsha: Chinyelu printing press, 1962) 64pp.
The school of love and how to attend it.
The Sorrows of Patrice Lumumba (Onitsha) 42 pp.
The temple of love.
The trials and death of Lumumba (Onitsha: Michael Allan Ohaejesi) 45 pp. ill. Th.
Uba, Eke
The broken heart (Enugu, Aut., 1958) 17 pp.
Romance in a nutshell (Enugu, 1959) 28 pp.
Ude, A. O.
Nigerian bachelor's guide.
Udeaga, M. O.
True confessions of a convent miss. 'Love in tragedy' (Okigwi: Solar Press publishers) 21 pp. Nar.
Umunnah, Cyril
They died in the game of love. 'Thony and his mother, Cathe and Agnes died for the sake of love making', Intr.: Robinson Dibua (Onitsha: Njoku & Sons Bookshop) 44 pp. Nar.
Uwadiegwu, C. O.
The complete story and works of Military Government and Nigerian current affairs.
The records of Northern and Western Crises in Nigeria.
Uwadoka, Lazarus
The roadside girl in misery, Intr.: S. Iroka (Aba: Aut.) 32 pp. Nar.
Uzoh, John E.
Love shall never end. 'The romance of love' (Onitsha: Njoku & Sons) 47 pp. Nar.
Uzoh, S.
Tribius and Folida.
Wosuagwu, P. P.
The death and burial of an aged man or oke amadi (according to Ntigha native custom).
My four years stay and experience of Ntigha town. (Agbani: Oteka Press) 34 pp. B.

Index